AF416358

Praise for Delivering the Digital Restaurant: The Path to Digital Maturity

"Independent restaurants and chains alike will gain practical tips to take the next step in their digital journey. A fantastic playbook that helps restaurants find their way through digitization. By the end of this book, you'll know how to master the off-premise channel…and your in-house business will benefit as a result."

— Bill Allen, Restaurateur & Investor

"An impartial, practical guide that helps restaurant owners and operators live through digitization. It's a marathon, not a sprint. Sandland and Orsbourn keep restaurateurs focused on doing the right next thing."

— Shawn Walchef, Founder, CaliBBQ Media

"Sandland and Orsbourn take restaurants on a path to a prosperous digital future."

— Christine Barone, Restaurant Industry Executive

"If you are struggling to manage the digital channel strategy for your restaurant, you need this book. As the perfect follow up to Delivering the Digital Restaurant: Your Roadmap to the Future of Food, which explained why restaurants must be digital, this book explains how to succeed digitally."

— *Alex Eagle, CEO Freebirds,*
Board Member, Texas Restaurant Association

"I've coached thousands of independent restaurant owners; I can confidently say many of them have the same questions about technology. They don't know where to start. This book explains the why and how in simple terms. It is a must-read for anyone who wants to take their restaurant to the next level. The tips scattered throughout the book can have an immediate impact on your business and your profits."

— *Donald Burns, The Restaurant Coach™*

"This book is a MUST READ for any technology innovator looking to be one step ahead of the wants and needs of their clients."

– *Michael "Schatzy" Schatzberg, Branded Hospitality Ventures,*
Restaurant & Technology Investor

Scan the code to visit DeliveringTheDigitalRestaurant.com

Connect with us on Social
Facebook: DeliveringTheDigitalRestaurant
Instagram: @thedigital.restaurant
LinkedIn: DeliveringTheDigitalRestaurant
TikTok: thedigitalrestaurant
Twitter: @LearnDelivery

Delivering the Digital Restaurant: The Path to Digital Maturity

Independently Published
www.DeliveringTheDigitalRestaurant.com

This edition printed in 2023.

Cover design by Westwords Consulting, LLC

For more information, please contact:
info@thedigital.restaurant

Library of Congress Control Number: 2023900139
ISBN: 979-8-9876668-1-4

Printed in the United States

DELIVERING
THE DIGITAL RESTAURANT
THE PATH TO DIGITAL MATURITY

MEREDITH SANDLAND | CARL ORSBOURN

TABLE OF CONTENTS

FOREWORD

When I first read Delivering the Digital Restaurant: Your Roadmap to the Future of Food, I was blown away. It laid the groundwork for explaining everything that has happened to our industry in the last few years and what is yet to come. It detailed the why and sounded the warning bell to those who were maintaining their old, analog ways.

What it didn't do was tell me what I needed to do next. This latest book from the award-winning authors provides the how. It completes their overall mission of arming restaurants with what they need to win in an off-premise market.

I've been in the restaurant industry for over 30 years: I studied hospitality at college and have worked for some of the biggest names in the business, such as TGI Fridays and The Cheesecake Factory. I thought I had seen everything, and then the pandemic hit. Keeping the business going while navigating the effects of the pandemic—during which time the entire industry was going through a digital disruption—was complex, to say the least. It soon became clear that those with the foresight to adopt digitization and the courage to innovate and test new approaches while stepping forward into the mire of confusion often caused by off-premise channels had an advantage.

Today, as the CEO of Alfa Co, I lead two casual dining brands, two fast-casual brands, a to-go snack concept, and a host of virtual brands across 88 locations in Saudi Arabia. Our company had that vision to invest in the future, and now, as the dust settles on a tumultuous period for our industry, I can reflect on where we are and where we are going.

This book helps each restaurateur define their own perspective and clearly articulates how restaurants can find their place on what the authors call a "path to digital maturity." I'm not sure there's a finish point on this journey, and the authors certainly don't imply there's a simple linear path or an imposed timeline to get there, but they do provide clear direction on where to focus during each step of the journey. The value of this book is that it creates a clear path for every restaurateur—independent or chain executive—AND every tech provider to question where they are and what their appetite is for moving to the next stage of maturity.

Everyone needs to know their starting level of off-premise competence to make the right decisions for their business. While robotics, artificial intelligence, and automation will continue to challenge us all to consider the future they offer, this book helps anyone involved in restaurants see where to focus now.

The wisdom within this book, much like that offered by its predecessor, will propagate throughout our industry in the decade ahead, establishing the foundational principles of what digital success is for restaurants. The exercises and helpful hints you will find within these pages translate what I loved about the first book into actionable decisions for each restaurant to consider. This book represents a perfect accompaniment to the first and a tool for those of us trying to stay ahead. I hope you enjoy it as much as I did and take steps to implement the suggestions that follow. Good luck.

Jonathan Norotsky
CEO, Alfa Co

INTRODUCTION

Kizzy was eager to get to the conference hall. She had spent the last 5 hours of her trip traveling from chilly Columbus to the warm, dry oasis of Phoenix, Arizona. It was the first time she had left the restaurant team at Kwixo on their own for three years, and she was understandably anxious. However, the excitement and anticipation of this conference overcame her anxiety. The conference had promised answers to questions about her business's technological future.

After dropping her bags in her room and calling the team back home to check how service went, she studied the agenda and saw that the exhibition hall had opened. She changed her shoes, reapplied her lipstick, and went downstairs.

Thirty minutes later, Kizzy stood in the center of the exhibition hall, wondering if the source of her exhaustion was her travels or the bewildering and overwhelming sight in front of her. She took in hundreds of exhibits and their 12-foot-high signs, video screens, and fun conference giveaways. She heard the voices of vendors reconnecting after months apart. And everyone was offering the reasons why they could help Kizzy and other operators like her. But right now, she thought to herself, "Where do I even start?"

As Kizzy walked down the row of exhibits to her left, she sequentially saw a loyalty provider, a feedback generation tool, an AI insights consultant, a text messaging service, a POS platform, a food supplier, a hygiene management software provider, a kiosk service, a delivery consolidator, a virtual restaurant licensor, an employee recruitment service, and a set of lockers with bright lights and a sign stating, "Your answer to labor & pick up solutions." "Yeah, right," she thought to herself. By now, she had more questions than answers. No one was there to guide her through how to determine what was most important for her restaurant—and who would even be prepared to help a small independent restaurant like hers?

The number one question we've received regarding the book *Delivering the Digital Restaurant: Your Roadmap to the Future of Food* is, "What is a digital restaurant?" Our answer? Being where your guests are, which increasingly is in the digital world. While this is a great guiding northstar, there are many different pieces required to become a fully digital restaurant.

Another frequently asked question is, "How do I decide what I need?" This issue has grown increasingly relevant to restaurant owners and operators since the pandemic. During COVID, many restaurateurs did whatever it took to survive, and successfully keep the lights on. Rapid decisions were made, procurement processes were less thorough, and for many, the off-premise channel became the savior that allowed them to stay in business.

As restaurants emerge from surviving the pandemic, and guests return to the restaurant, the power and potential of an off-premise channel remains. The potential for a restaurant to grow sales has never been as high—especially as they now exist in a less competitive environment where many didn't survive. But that potential has been dampened by the complexity of necessary short-term decisions that resulted in a complex stack of technology, collectively adding sizable costs to the equation. The time is right for restaurants to revisit their digital strategy, review and take stock of their progress, and plot a path towards digital success across all the channels they serve.

While the technology choices for a restaurant may seem daunting, breaking the process down into concrete steps to digital maturity can help limit that complexity

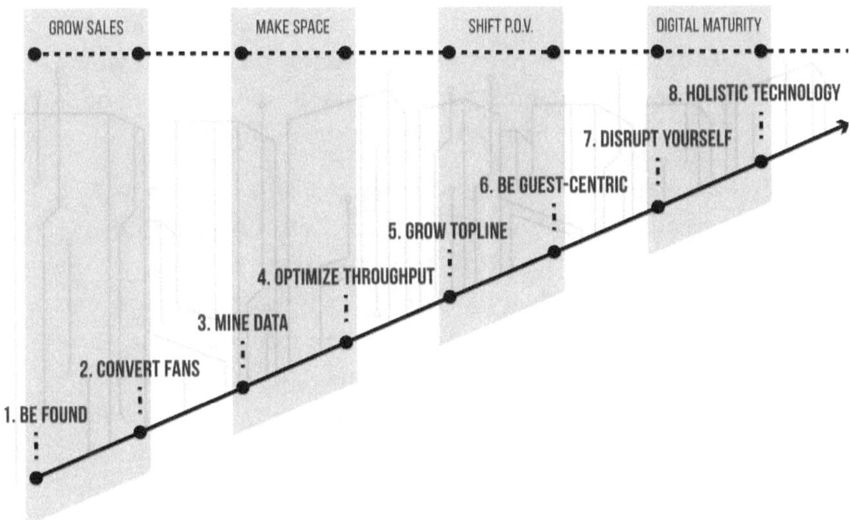

The Path to Digital Maturity

and focus the decision-making process on what's important now. Restaurants can take advantage of digitally enabled growth without getting bogged down by all of the choices that need to be made to reach full digital maturity.

But first, what is digital maturity? A fully mature digital restaurant is one that takes advantage of all the technology tools available. It also represents an awareness of your restaurant's true output capacity, the knowledge of what tools are needed when to drive further uplift and efficiency, and having a great handle on data across all parts of your restaurant—from your ingredients to each guest's specific needs. The path to digital maturity involves the process of adding in functionality to become a fully digital restaurant and understanding when you're ready to make the next step on the journey. We think of this evolution as a seven-step process, which can be broken down into the four key sections that make up this book.

1. **Grow Sales:** As we saw throughout the pandemic, digitization proved key to restaurant survival and growth and continues to enable restaurants to grow sales through off-premise transactions. However, there is far more to that undertaking than facilitating off-premise transactions. Understanding how to get the most from third-

party marketplaces and having a clear plan to migrate customers to first-party direct ordering are the areas where most restaurants must focus. We'll talk about driving both third-party and first-party in chapters 1 and 2.

2. **Make Space:** The digital tools available today generate incredible data. Once a restaurant sells through multiple channels, they gain the opportunity to optimize profit by mastering this data. Used wisely, such data can focus sales and operations on the most profitable parts of the business. Further, this data can be used to shape improved forecasting and improved execution. New sales channels and improved operations can translate into increased sales. Unfortunately, this process has revealed a new problem—the restaurant can't cope with all the extra sales it now generates. At this stage, restaurateurs must consider the kitchen design and processes within them. We'll talk about using data to optimize sales and operations and then dissect how best to hone in on operational excellence in chapters 3 and 4.

3. **Shift POV** (Point of View): With this new capacity in mind, we'll look at what the most advanced restaurants are doing, and how a shift in perspective can help restaurants serve their best customers more frequently. By understanding that a guest can exist across a multitude of channels and then tracking that guest across all channels, restaurants can be as informed today as they have ever been about who they serve. Building an operation that services the "known" guest enables new ways to harness the new capacity. Once embraced as a point of view, restaurants can be built differently, and their success can be assessed differently. We'll talk about utilizing capacity effectively to serve the guest in chapters 5 and 6.

4. **Digital Maturity:** In Chapters 7 & 8, we'll describe the most forward-thinking restaurants, that start at the end of the journey and work backward. This strategy enables these restaurants to benefit even further from their technology—not just through integration, but also through

holistic restaurant technology that coordinates and optimizes resources throughout the consumer and product journeys. While most restaurants are adding technology in phases, a few have decided to start with a blank slate, asking themselves, "If what consumers want is delivered food, what is the best way to make that happen?" At this stage in the maturity path, a restaurant has all the technology solutions it needs and has integrated them all together. As the restaurant continues to innovate, it must focus on improving the execution and differentiating service. The very best digitally native restaurants build and assemble tech stacks that seamlessly fit together. The very best keep ahead by continually reinvesting to take advantage of the newest technologies.

Your restaurant may wish to work on the immediate next step only—and for that this book is a great guide. Or your restaurant may wish to start at the end and work backward—and for that this book will describe all the pieces your holistic solution requires to be successful.

A note of caution: Proceeding in this linear fashion can mean that decisions made today may affect options available to your restaurant tomorrow. The best way to keep future options open is to ensure you are selecting modern software that has an "Open API" structure—meaning that it plays well with

Tips are highlighted throughout the book.

- Tips will help you focus on best practices that may make sense for your restaurant.
- Tips reflecting what your restaurant is already doing suggests you are ready to go to the next phase.
- Tips that are new to your restaurant may suggest where to focus now before going on to more advanced stages of the journey.

other functionality that you may later add. The more a piece of software claims to have an "ecosystem of partners," especially if they have multiple partners that offer similar functionality, the more likely it is to integrate into your future roadmap easily. Technology integrations are otherwise a bottleneck to a restaurant's ability to increase its speed toward digital maturity.

APIs have their limits. We'll end the book by speaking directly to the technologists—the weight of technology for restaurant owners must become lighter. Chapter 8 describes the emerging technology platforms that eliminate resources and cost from restaurant executives that have been working hard to choose technology partners, integrate the choices they've made, and make the best of a variety of different tools.

TIME FOR REFLECTION!

- Apply what you have learned in this chapter.
- Answer the questions below or go to your downloaded workbook and answer the chapter questions about YOUR business.
- If you have not done so yet, the workbook can be downloaded for FREE in an easy-to-use format at our website at DeliveringTheDigitalRestaurant.com/ThePath

Our first book, *Delivering the Digital Restaurant: Your Roadmap to the Future of Food,* is a good introduction to what follows here. That first book introduces many of the terms and concepts used in this book and details many of the underlying reasons for the change the restaurant industry is currently experiencing. We hope this companion book complements our first, lengthier text in helping restaurants and the amazing entrepreneurs behind them find their spot on the path to digital maturity and move forward confidently in the months and years ahead toward digital success.

At the end of every chapter, we'll invite you to answer some questions to help validate where your restaurant is on the path to digital maturity and areas in which some self-reflection could help drive improvements. Take time to answer these, speak with your team members and be as honest as possible. Where you sense any bias for your business kicking in, reach out to a fellow restaurant colleague and ask them to help you provide an honest view. Not all tips and adjustments make sense for your particular restaurant—each brand is different. Asking these questions will help you apply the concepts in this book to your restaurant in a way that is right for your brand. These worksheets can be downloaded for FREE in an easy-to-use format at our website at DeliveringTheDigitalRestaurant.com/ThePath

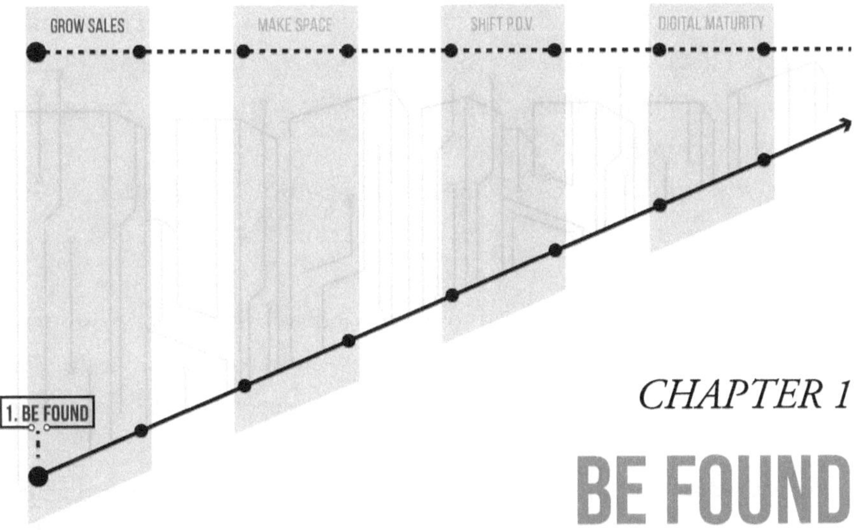

CHAPTER 1

BE FOUND

Raj scanned the app on his phone, scrolling down with flicks of his right thumb on the screen. He had just signed up for the free delivery service for a year, thanks to his credit card. He loved the convenience of using the app, especially as there just seemed to be more and more restaurants added all the time. Today, though, he was making a bigger order. The guys were heading over to watch the big game, and he just didn't have time to head to the grocery store to get the beers and the chips he thought he had. So, he decided to order some food for delivery and get a few cases of cold Heinekens in for the crew.

"Nope…no…no…maybe…bad…ooooh, tried it last week, but Mo won't like it," he thought to himself, discounting the options as he went through his home screen's list.

He glanced at his watch and realized he didn't have long. The guys would be showing up any time now, and the game started in just 35 minutes. "Best make this quick," he concluded.

His gaze returned to the app and the banner that said "Fastest Near You." Hotdogs, burgers, chicken wings—loads of options. Raj settled on the restaurant that offered American comfort food at a 20 percent reduction over a spend of $40. "I'll easily spend that with the way these guys eat," he smirked. Within a few seconds, he was building his order.

He put his phone to the side, turned on the TV, found the appropriate channel, and ramped up the volume. Just as he sat down to listen to the pre-game commentary, the doorbell rang.

"Let's get this party started," he said as he rushed downstairs to greet his first guest.

Almost every restaurant that survived the pandemic relied upon third-party marketplaces. If your restaurant isn't on any of the marketplaces, chances are you don't trust a third-party, with its fees and independent drivers, to give your guests the experience you want to deliver with your brand.

For everyone else, these marketplaces are a great place to start because, without any investment, they make your restaurant available to online guests, including those who may not have been thinking about your brand while they were thinking about their hunger. The marketplaces are specialized search engines—Google for restaurant food, Amazon for prepared meal

Tip: Marketplaces are search engines.

- Hungry people who aren't sure what to eat go to marketplaces to see what's available.

- Restaurants on the marketplaces are competing for the same digital real estate.

- Gear all your decisions towards maximizing your searchability; consult an SEO specialist if you aren't sure how to do this.

- Restaurant and menu item names must be easily understandable by a computer algorithm.

- Tag your restaurant with categories that will make it both findable and competitive.

- Consumers "flicking through" the app must have an instant attraction to your food—great professional photography really matters.

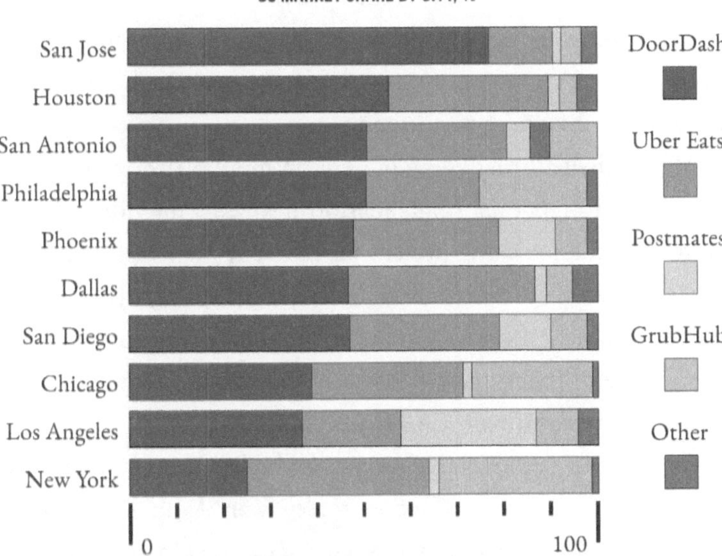

Source: https://www.mckinsey.com/industries/technology-media-and-telecommunications/our-insights/ordering-in-the-rapid-evolution-of-food-delivery

Figure 1.1 US Food Delivery Market Share by City

shopping. When hungry, convenience-seeking guests aren't sure what they want for dinner, they look on the marketplaces.

Set up is easy; orders start to flow in, and the ecosystem of drivers delivers the meals. What could be better? While turning on a marketplace is easy, doing well as a restaurant on a marketplace requires putting time and attention into making proactive decisions about how your restaurant will work with these third parties.

1. How many marketplaces should your brand be on?

Our default answer is "all of them." But if the answer isn't all of them, which marketplace should you choose? DoorDash currently has the highest US market share, so it seems logical to choose that one. The problem is, while DoorDash has strong national market share, Uber Eats, Grubhub, or Postmates may be the strongest local provider in your city. Before selecting just one marketplace, survey your consumers, consult the internet, and ask your marketplace rep about local market share.

As apparent from the "market share by city" graph above from McKinsey & Company, being on just DoorDash in San Jose would probably work for a restaurant, but being on only this platform in New York City would lead to sub-optimal online sales performance.

Generally, we believe that being present on more platforms is better. Each consumer tends to rely on a single platform, so reaching different segments of consumers demands being present on different marketplaces. "We coach restaurants to turn on all five [delivery marketplaces]," says Toast CEO Chris Comparato. "Some of them may be more profitable, some of them may have lower fees, some of them may offer you more data, and some may be more convenient [to the consumer] on a Friday night."[1]

Similarly, consider your niche of food and whether cuisine-oriented marketplaces are also a fit. Chowbus, for example, is an Asian food marketplace. Since its inception in 2016, founders Suyu Zhang and Linxin Wen have found great success targeting Asian restaurateurs and customers that specifically want Asian food across two continents—North America and Australia.

The more marketplaces your restaurant is on, the more your restaurant will need an aggregator. Aggregators do exactly what the term implies—they consolidate orders originating in all channels so that all marketplace orders come to the restaurant in a single stream. If your restaurant is still living with multiple tablets, add an aggregator. Chowly, Deliverect, Ordermark, and Otter all solve this problem. Increasingly, several POS companies will aggregate directly without another piece of software in between. "We hear from restaurants that streamlining order management so that everything flows through their POS is crucial for efficient operations, but this is table stakes," said Zhong Xu, CEO of Deliverect. "To help restaurants attract more customers and improve margins, they need solutions that boost store availability, publish compelling and accurate menus in real-time, and streamline kitchen operations."

Importantly, the better aggregators also perform accounting reconciliation at the transaction level. Meaning, for any chargebacks a marketplace puts to your restaurant, the aggregator can assign that chargeback to a specific original transaction—which makes it far easier for your restaurant to figure out if the chargeback is appropriate. If it isn't appropriate, your restaurant has a specific order to refer to with the marketplace and can precisely define the difference.

Tip: Aggregators reduce stress on the kitchen.

- Ensure orders from marketplaces are not "re-keyed" manually into a POS to reduce errors.
- Combine marketplace orders into one order stream to help the kitchen prioritize.
- Aggregators can push the order stream into your KDS (kitchen display system) to ensure all orders are put directly through to the kitchen.
- Cooks will have fewer headaches if they have fewer beeps to respond to.

For example, if the consumer did not receive their drink, the drink in the order should be refunded—not the entire order. If the chargeback is appropriate, your restaurant operations can determine how to remedy the issue to prevent it from happening again. Yadavan Mahendraraj of Uber Eats says, "We agree transparency is critical in building strong partnerships, and as a result of feedback from partners we've improved order error reports to make it easier to reconcile to the transaction, understand what went wrong, and reach out to the customer to make it right. Our best partners then take the data we make available to adjust their processes, menus, and staffing levels to decrease order errors."

Digitally mature restaurants have a clearly defined process for managing chargebacks and addressing the root cause. Chargebacks in the 2 to 4 percent of sales range are not uncommon. If your two-million-dollar restaurant is doing 10 percent of sales in delivery (two hundred thousand dollars), then chargebacks could be eating four to eight thousand dollars in profit each year.

2. Which tier of service should your restaurant choose on each marketplace?

DoorDash, Uber Eats, and Grubhub have all introduced pricing tiers that charge different commissions to restaurants that value different outcomes. While the tiers differ slightly on each marketplace, they all share the same underlying philosophy: pay more to get more. Choosing which tier to use on each platform is the first major decision your restaurant will make.

Tip: Track your spend on marketplaces.

- Marketplace costs fall into four categories: commissions, advertising spend, promotional costs, and chargebacks. Track each one separately to manage each cost independently.

- Commissions are a cost of doing business with the marketplaces that are netted against revenue in the P&L, but you may think of them as a marketing cost because you are using them to acquire customers.

- Advertising spend is squarely a marketing cost.

- Promotional costs (e.g., discounted food, free deliveries) affect the food margin in the P&L but should also be considered as part of the total marketing cost.

- When creating your LTV:CAC ratio (discussed in Chapter 3) you will need to take into account all customer acquisition costs, regardless of where they fall in the P&L (commissions, ad spend, promo costs).

- Restaurants can have the most impact on chargebacks through careful monitoring and great operations.

It is critical to think of third-party marketplaces as a virtual food court. Hungry consumers are going there. Do you want your brand to be a choice they easily find? Restaurants typically pay higher rents to be in a busy, Class-A mall food court than they would pay to be streetside in a low-traffic, not very densely populated environment. The commission structures work the same way. The more online traffic likely to see your restaurant as an option in their search, the higher the commission structure. The less online traffic, the lower. In a similar way, paying more "online rent" in the form of a higher commission puts your restaurant in front of more consumers. "Third-party is here to stay, particularly among Gen Z. They do DoorDash. They do Uber Eats. It's part of their dining culture," says Barry Shuster of RestaurantOwner.com. "Third-party is a good marketing tool because people are using them. If you aren't on them, you are losing revenue and losing visibility."[2]

Larger brands sometimes have more leeway in negotiating fees and services provided with third-party platforms. This can seem frustrating for smaller, independent restaurants, who are typically funneled through the standard pricing tiers. The logic for the platforms is twofold: first, is your brand well-known enough that it is bringing consumers to the platform (vs. the platform bringing consumers to the brand)? Second, does your brand generate enough sales on the platform to be worth a custom pricing conversation for both parties? For large, national brands, the answer to both these questions is "yes," opening the door to a discussion about what the fees should be. For

	DOORDASH (DD)	UBER EATS (UE)	GRUBHUB (GH)
SELF-DELIVERY	• 12% • Option to use DD drivers for $6 per delivery	• 15% • Option to use UE drivers for another 10%	• 8%
BASIC TIER	• 15% for delivery • 6% for pickup • Basic listing on DD platform	• 15% for delivery • 6% for pickup • Only visible to consumers searching by brand name	• 18% for delivery (5% marketing + 3% CC processing + 10% delivery) • Basic listing on GH platform • Higher diner delivery fees
MIDDLE TIER	• 25% for delivery • 6% for pickup • Access to Dashpass guests • Larger delivery radius	• 25% for delivery • 6% for pickup • Basic listing on UE platform • Access to Uber One users	• 20-30% for delivery • Medium diner delivery fees • Access to Grubhub+ diners
PREMIUM TIER	• 30% for delivery • 6% for pickup • Revenue guarantee	• 30% for delivery • 6% for pickup • Prioritized listing on home screen and in search results • Revenue guarantee	• 33% for delivery • Medium diner delivery fees • Access to loyalty and promotions tools • Ability to respond to reviews • Lowest diner delivery fees

Figure 1.2 Merchant Charges by Tier by Platform

smaller, single-location brands, the answer is likely to be at best "sort of," which keeps the door to negotiations closed.

Looking at these options is dizzying. For an independent restaurant on all three platforms, we'd suggest starting at the premium tier to build your restaurant's base of reviews and get your restaurants into consumers' re-order carousel. Then, over time, you can choose whether this premium tier continues to make sense for your restaurant. We'll come back to this idea when we get to the capacity section of the digital maturity model, but it is critical to remember your restaurant is paying a premium (30 percent!) to be in this busy, Class-A digital mall. Make every transaction count by delivering great product in a short order-to-delivery time. Revisit Chapter 11 "Operating in a Virtual World" in *Delivering the Digital Restaurant*, which details the importance of great off-premise operations in accuracy, speed, and quality if required. It does not make sense to pay a premium only to disappoint guests.

Remember, the commission is just one part of how the marketplaces make money. While the third-party marketplaces are charging your restaurant a percentage of the total ticket, they are also charging consumers service fees and delivery fees (and keeping them rather than passing them back to you). The DoorDash service fee varies from 8 to 19 percent of the total ticket, meaning

 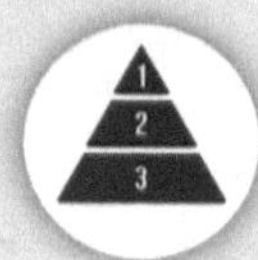

Tip: Getting to first place.

- Starting your restaurant on the premium tier with a marketplace can help jump-start sales.

- Your restaurant may not always need to be on the premium tier; monitor search results to see whether or not your restaurant is easy to find.

- An increasing portion of platform sales are coming from their customers that have opted in to their membership programs (UberOne, DashPass, Grubhub+); these customers are unlikely to switch to your restaurant's direct ordering channels so the middle tier of service may always be required to access these customers.

that a consumer is paying total prices that are 8 to 19 percent higher than what your brand charges. The delivery fee is typically $1.99 to $5.99, depending on the type of restaurant, the distance from restaurant to consumer, any promotions the restaurant or the platform may be running, and the timing of the delivery (on- vs. off-peak). The third-party marketplace determines this delivery fee, and any discounts (e.g., "free delivery" offers) are funded by the restaurant through promotional advertising fees paid to the marketplace.

Finally, the third-party marketplaces ask consumers to pay a tip to the driver. As much as all of the above fees may cause restaurants heartache, the tip can cause restaurant staff just as much strife. Tips to drivers go 100 percent to drivers and are not split with the marketplace or the restaurant staff. While many restaurants pool tips and share them with back-of-house workers, the third-party marketplaces have no provision for tip-splitting or even for the consumer to send a separate tip straight to the restaurant staff.

Let's look at the charges from the perspective of the marketplace, the consumer, the driver, and the restaurant. In this example, the consumer is paying 76 percent more than they would to dine in at a fast casual that accepts no tips. That money is split between the driver and the marketplace—which makes sense because these two parties made this digital order and delivery happen. The remaining $8.99 per order in this example goes to the market-place. While that seems like a large amount, the marketplace needs to pay for credit card processing, fund tech R&D, guest acquisition, and overhead out of this revenue, which is why most marketplaces in most cities are still losing money. As the marketplaces slow down their rate of tech investment, restaurants adopt the platforms, consumers adopt the platforms, and delivery density increases, the marketplaces start to make more money city by city.

Meanwhile, consumers will always pay more, and restaurants will get less than they would have had the transaction been a traditional dine-in transaction because of the structure of developed restaurant markets. In developing markets that have "skipped the landline" to go straight to ghost kitchens, kitchen automation, and low-cost delivery, restaurants can make more, and consumers pay less in a delivery transaction. It seems hard to believe—but more developed markets will get there. More on this later when we discuss the digitally native restaurants that are emerging.

	Consumer Dining In	Consumer Pays for delivery	Marketplace gets for delivery	Restaurant gets for delivery	Driver gets for delivery
Menu price	$25	$30 (Most restaurants mark-up vs. dine-in)	$9 (30%)	$21	N/A
Service fee (15%)	$0	$4.50	$4.5	$0	$0 (+possible bonuses)
Delivery fee	$0	$4.99	$4.99	$0	$5 (can be $2-10 depending on time, distance, and tip potential)
Tip (15%)	$0	$4.50	$0	$0	$4.50
Total	$25	$42.99 (76% more than dining in)	$18.49 - payments to driver = $8.99 - credit card processing = $7.41	$21 (16% less than dining in)	$9.50

*omits taxes

Figure 1.3 Delivery Charges by Marketplace Participant

3. How much should your restaurant charge on the third-party platforms?

"I just increase my prices by 43 percent to accommodate the 30 percent these marketplaces are taking" is a sentence we hear often. While price increases might work for national brands that have a known value position with consumers, they run the risk of hurting local brands that are relatively unknown off-platform. The menu prices on the marketplaces become the menu prices in consumers' minds, and they may choose to avoid dining in at your restaurant if they perceive it to be dramatically more expensive than it truly is. Here, we'd tread lightly.

If you plan to increase your menu prices on the marketplaces, take a look at your local competitors on the marketplaces to ensure you have not priced yourself out of consideration. Most national brands, when they do increase prices on the marketplaces, do so by only 15 to 25 percent. The most sophisticated national brands keep menu prices fairly similar but offer incentives for first-party ordering and pickup that are not available on the marketplaces.

4. How do you get your restaurant prioritized on the platform to ensure it's in the consumer consideration set?

There are three objectives for your restaurant on the platforms:

1. Be on the homepage (the first destination for a hungry consumer looking for food).

2. Be above the fold on the homepage or at least in your category (a consumer can see your restaurant without scrolling).

3. Be in the carousels (<30 minutes, promotions, ordered previously).

Tip: Be fast.

- Search engine algorithms care about what consumers train them to care about.

- Marketplace algorithms reward speed, ratings, price, deals, and customer conversion.

- Increase speed by reducing maketime in the merchant portal to 10 minutes or less, eliminating complex items, and increasing throughput capability (more on this in Chapter 4).

- Marketplaces add 20 minutes for delivery = An 11-minute or greater maketime removes the restaurant from the 30-minute carousel.

- Improve ratings by only offering menu items your team can consistently execute well. Consider removing items from your delivery menu if they are garnering poor reviews.

Achieving these objectives is easiest and cheapest with great operations. Strong ratings, reasonable prices, and short delivery times will cause consumers to click on your restaurant. The more clicks and orders your restaurant receives, the more the platform will prioritize your restaurant in its search results.

The second easiest (and also free!) way to get your restaurant noticed is to ensure your menu item titles and descriptions line up with typical consumer search terms. Treat your page like the front entrance of your restaurant and your menu design. Keep it clean, compelling, and inviting. If you haven't yet invested in quality photography, do so. Your guests, as the saying goes, eat with their eyes. High-end photography with consistent backdrops and angled (not top-down) photography celebrating the food (and not the trimmings around the plate) are important.

After that, it's time to start spending money. Offering promotions and spending on sponsored results on the platforms is a great way to get your brand noticed. Getting that first order will then put your brand in the "ordered previously" carousel. Experimentation is critical here. Measuring the success of which carousels work and which do not is important to determine what works for your restaurant in your market. If you have multiple units of similar profiles, try A/B testing your carousels, with one unit trying

Tip: Flex, but don't stop, marketing spend.

- Focus your marketing spend on times when the platforms aren't promoting you naturally.

- Don't spend while the platforms are promoting you as "new to platform."

- Do spend once the platforms remove their support.

- Marketing spend on platform is one of the attributes that feeds the algorithms.

- Once your restaurant is "in the carousels" you may not need to spend as much, but be sure to always spend something.

one carousel and the other trying an alternative. If you have only one unit, test each carousel in sequence—one at a time—to isolate changes.

5. Should your restaurant pay for advertising on the marketplaces, in addition to the commissions it's already paying?

Advertising on the marketplaces has grown tremendously over the last year. YipitData reports the offers available have increased over 40 percent[3]. The platforms report tremendous ROI on marketing spend, and one of the best things about it is that your team can directly correlate advertising spend to consumer spend.

Delivery marketing master Andre Vener of Dog Haus thinks a steady state of marketing spend on the platforms is 10 percent of platform revenue. "When you are new to a platform, the platform will promote your restaurant. You don't need to spend. After a few weeks, when the platform stops promoting your restaurant as new, then the marketing spend needs to kick in. Then, once consumers have found your restaurant, you can back off."[4] Alonso Castanada, marketing partner at Savory Restaurant Fund, cautions not to back off too far. "Just be sure to always spend something," he says, "even if it's only $1 to 2 per week per location so the algorithms don't forget you."[5]

6. Is there another place to be found?

While the third-party marketplaces are an important customer acquisition channel, there is another, less talked-about channel that may be even better. Third-party marketplaces are a miniscule element in customer engagement rates when compared to search engine usage. 68 percent of online experiences begin with a search engine.[6] Most notably, Google represents a dormant giant in guest acquisition potential and restaurants can and should use SEO (search engine optimization) tactics to ensure their restaurant is findable and high up in search results. Because Google represents 94 percent of all mobile search traffic,[7] if a customer is hungry, they may well ask Google about where to eat before they ask a marketplace. Particularly with features like "search near me" and Google Maps, hungry customers turn to Google to find out how to satiate their hunger quickly. Just like with customers on a marketplace, Google searchers are not window shoppers—they want to be fed.

A Backlinko study in 2019 found that a Google search result for a business

Tip: Maintain your website.

- Static and old content hurts your search result ranking.
- Updated, new content helps your search result ranking.
- Claim your "Google my Business" page and make sure it is accurate.
- Respond to Google reviews (both positive and negative) regularly.
- Consider automatically updating your website with content from other sources (e.g.,Instagram, TikTok).

at #1 in the ranking had a CTR (click-through rate) of 27.6 percent, some 10 times better than those ranked in the tenth position.[8] Even if you can't get your restaurant to #1 in the listing, the same study showed that moving up one spot still yields an improvement of relative CTR by 32.3 percent. However, if you're on the second page of Google results, only 0.63 percent of searchers will ever click on your website. The same study found that for those advertising on Google, longer key words (10 to 15 words) tend to perform better (29.2 percent CTR) than single-word terms (16.5 percent) because they imply a particular search intent that is clearly quite specific. This means "Italian Restaurants near the train station" may work better than simply "Italian Restaurants." Using Google's keyword planner is a handy tool to learn what your guests are searching for when they are on the search engine.

There are entire books that outline how to improve your Google ranking, but the basics are pretty clear. Most of this is possible through managing your Google Business profile appropriately and having a dynamic home page with frequent content changes to maintain fresh and compelling content. Google's algorithms reward content, reviews, and engagement.

Investing time in your Google search results carries some real benefit to your restaurant's discoverability. It will help your customers find your restaurant for every occasion, but you will need to consider an important issue: where do you want them to go once they've found you? If they reserve a table, should it be on OpenTable, Resy, Tock, or your own reservation platform? If they order food for delivery, should it be through Google Order, a third-party marketplace, or your own direct, first-party ordering channel?

Google food ordering sits halfway between the third-party marketplaces and first-party ordering. Like the marketplaces, Google charges a commission, albeit lower than those charged by the marketplaces. However, just as is the case with the marketplaces, Google is the primary beneficiary of the consumer behavioral data, and Google food ordering makes it just as easy for customers to first find and then order from your restaurant. If your restaurant lacks a strong first-party ordering channel, Google food ordering is a great option to increase sales at reduced fees compared to the marketplaces without the hassle of setting up technology infrastructure. If your restaurant has a strong first-party ordering channel, you'll want your Google search result to link directly to your own ordering site.

How your restaurant routes customers from a Google search is crucial—every step a guest makes from that point on may indoctrinate their ongoing behavior as they engage with your restaurant. Will it be through third-party interfaces—which in turn takes them a step away from being your guest—or through your own channels? We'll explore this topic in detail in the next chapter.

Summary: Be Found

- Third-party marketplaces play a critical role in the world of digital restaurants.

- Some customers will always choose marketplaces over any other method of ordering. To reach these customers, your restaurant must be on the marketplaces that are relevant in your area.

- Some customers can be compelled to switch to first-party, and for these, the third-party marketplaces serve as a customer acquisition tool.

- Optimize your presence on the marketplaces to drive sales to your restaurant: on the front page, above the fold, in the carousels.

- Consider pricing your marketplace menus higher than your direct and in-store channels, but watch how your competition prices so you don't become uncompetitive.

- Treat your marketplace page like the front entrance of your restaurant and like your menu design: keep it clean and make it compelling and inviting.

- Invest marketing spend to appear early in a consumer's search and always maintain some (even if it is minuscule) marketing spend on the platforms.

- SEO matters. Learn how to optimize or invest in ensuring your restaurant appears high up in Google's search results against the appropriate keywords and local searches.

  # TIME FOR REFLECTION!

CHAPTER 1: BE FOUND

1. Check your merchant portals across the marketplaces your restaurant participates in. What maketime is set? Can you reduce it to 10 minutes or less?

Platform	Maketime
1	
2	
3	
4	
5	
6	
7	
8	
9	
10	

2. Spot-check the production times for your delivery menu's 10 top-selling items from the last month.

Item	Product Mix (% of Sales)	Production Time
1		
2		
3		
4		
5		
6		
7		
8		
9		
10		

3. What action can you take this week to help reduce the production time of the top-selling items that take more than 10 minutes to produce?

4. During the peak time of business for your restaurants, create a new customer profile in each marketplace as if you were a guest who lives at an address nearby.

How far down the home page is your restaurant? First result? 17th? Repeat the process in your restaurant's primary category, then repeat the process in each major carousel.

Platform	Homepage Result	Category Result	# of Appearances in Carousels

5. Which carousels does your restaurant appear on? Which carousels are the most effective for your restaurant? Are they different in different marketplaces? What do you notice about the results?

6. What is your chargeback percent of sales by platform? How does this affect your restaurant's overall bottom line?

7. Have you developed a process to regularly monitor the chargebacks your restaurant receives? How can you improve operations to prevent chargebacks? What actions can you take to improve the chargeback recovery process?

8. What percent of platform sales are you reinvesting into marketing? How does this compare to the recommended 10 percent?

9. Where is your restaurant on Google rankings? When you type in its name and location where it resides? If you type in what you think a customer might be looking for if they didn't know your restaurant's name? What steps must you take to improve the ranking?

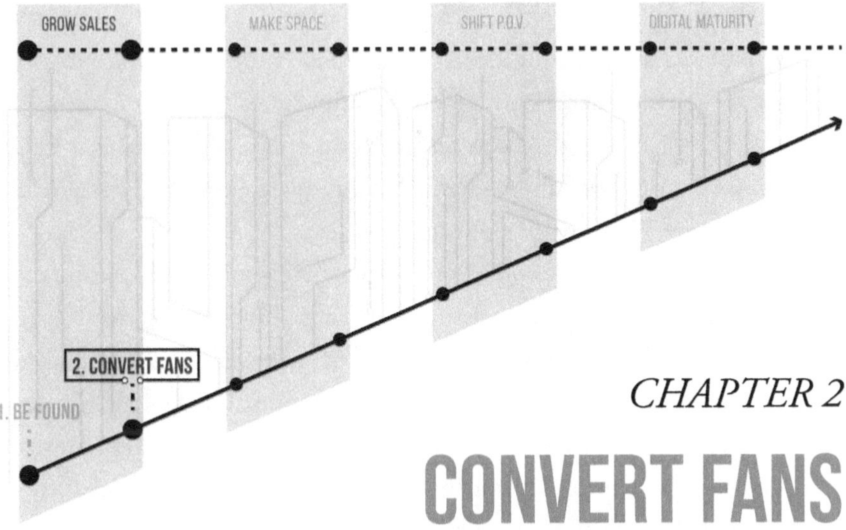

CHAPTER 2

CONVERT FANS

"I just don't know how you do it," sighed Kizzy.

She was sipping on her iced latte as she sat next to her lifelong friend and fellow restaurateur, Kevyn, whose restaurant was located just a few miles away. Their regular monthly coffee meeting was something they both looked forward to, and the cafe was a convenient midpoint between their restaurants.

"It's quite simple, Kizzy. You have to spend more to make more," Kevyn explained.

Kizzy shot back angrily, "How can I spend more when I'm already paying them such extortionate fees?" She continued, "And how are you getting people to order direct? No one even knows we switched that thing on."

Kevyn smiled gently and delicately placed his cup on the table. "The fees give you the keys, but you still need to put gas in the car. Thousands of restaurants are paying the same fee, but you have to do more to be found—and how much spend do you put into telling your current guests, yes, even your dine-in guests, about why it's worth their time to order direct and use your app so you don't even have to worry about the fees?"

A silent, almost uncomfortable moment passed as the two friends contemplated what to say next. Kizzy reached for her phone, clearly intent on showing her friend something important. A few more seconds passed, then Kizzy said, "Look at this. John's place sells similar cuisine and has one of these direct channels you talk about." She shook her phone in Kevyn's direction. "Please, look at it."

Kevyn took the phone and patiently spent a few minutes browsing the ordering process for the competitor that Kizzy had highlighted. Kevyn nodded, sighed, and mumbled under his breath until finally he looked up. "Kizzy—yes, he has a direct ordering channel, but look at it more functionally. There are so many things wrong with it. It takes an age to sign up, the photos are not the right size for the screen, and there's nothing slick or fast about using this. Where's Apple or Google Pay? I would stick to Uber Eats over this any day. This is not the model to follow. Take a look at my mobile ordering." He navigated to his own restaurant's page. Smiling as he handed Kizzy's phone back, Kevyn said, "I think this is something like what you need."

Kizzy returned the smile, thinking these monthly coffee catch-ups might need to happen more frequently.

Once a restaurant is on the third-party marketplaces, two things become obvious:

1. There is demand: Guests really do want the convenience of ordering digitally and eating off-premise.
2. There is a better way: Inserting a third-party between restaurant and guest increases cost for everyone and may lead to sub-optimal outcomes in the process.

The pandemic created a race to get restaurants online. As the only way to connect with guests became digital, almost every restaurant that survived the pandemic created a digital interface with its guests. You may recall Noah Glass of Olo saying in our first book he viewed his company as a "lifeboat" for restaurants during the pandemic. Olo's teams worked long hours to create a direct link to guests and took on many restaurants that didn't necessarily fit their target profile to get as many restaurants as possible through the shutdown and help them endure subsequent guest discomfort with public spaces.

Other direct-to-consumer ordering interfaces were no different. Restaurant technology (RestTech) funding from venture capitalists accelerated to new highs during the pandemic, reaching $2.3 billion in 2021—almost 30 percent more than pre-pandemic.[9] Online website and ordering companies like Popmenu, Lunchbox, and BentoBox raised significant rounds on relatively small revenue to explode in growth as they brought restaurants online. Even third-party platforms themselves, like DoorDash, have used their vast resources to help restaurants offer first-party ordering. The DoorDash system is called Storefront, and offers restaurants a zero-commission way to rapidly offer online ordering.

Restaurants, as one of the last industries to digitize, were quick to realize that if guests wanted to order online, restaurants could not just cede their guest relationships to third parties. "Look for first-party when it's available to you," says Toast CEO Comparato. "This is why we offer TDS [Toast Delivery Services] so that the restaurant wins back the guest and wins back the delivery fees. You're going to save yourself a lot in fees and gain yourself really rich data." TDS enables first-party ordering and offers a variety of logistics fulfillment methods on the back end. All the guest and ordering data is available to the restaurant using the platform.

Cali BBQ Media, a restaurant based in San Diego, California—whose founder, Shawn Walchef, has also made it a mission to share with other restaurants his digitization journey—uses Toast for just this reason.

> We live in an Amazon Prime world. Everything is about convenience and time. It's our job to remove friction. A mobile-first site that allows them to order directly from us. And that's why we chose Toast. I don't have to email someone to get our website updated. I don't have a Frankenstein of a tech stack.[10]

All first-party ordering systems save money in fees and preserve the guest relationship directly with the restaurant, generating data in the process. But just having a first-party ordering system does not automatically result in a

- Having a direct-ordering channel is not enough; the direct-ordering channel must be as easy for a customer to use as a platform is.

- Customers will not jump through hoops to order direct from your restaurant.

- Ordering, payments, and loyalty must be integrated, with as few clicks and data-entry points as possible.

- No amount of discounting will incentivize any but the most promotionally-oriented customer to do something hard.

lot of first-party orders. While most restaurants are lucky to get 10 to 20 percent of their digital orders direct, leading digital restaurants keep 75 to 95 percent of their digital orders direct. Restaurants need to follow their lead in understanding what it takes to keep guests ordering first-party.

As popular as the third parties are, there is also a significant market for direct guest ordering.

"Third-party is a channel that works for guest acquisition," says restaurant marketer Rev Ciancio. "But you have to have a system built for conversion to first-party."[11] By system, Ciancio means everything that goes into acquiring and keeping a guest as a first-party guest. Many restaurants mistakenly believe that offering an incentive to switch—like offering a discount or free item for ordering first-party—is enough. The problem is that guests are paying a premium to order third-party for a reason: it's so easy. If restaurants don't make it just as easy to order from them first-party as it is to order from them third-party, guests won't do it.

Before spending marketing dollars to encourage guests to make the move over to first-party, make sure that the first-party ordering experience is fantastic. Take the time to order from Chipotle, Panera, Starbucks, Sweetgreen, and Wingstop. These leaders have mastered the "capability triangle" for first-party ordering—digital ordering, payment, and loyalty.

Figure 2.1 The Capability Triangle

Digital Ordering

Getting digital ordering right means optimizing the experience for an online transaction. Don't just upload your existing menu and call it a day. Think through what guests want to do and how they interact with your team members in-restaurant. For example, if your guests frequently modify their orders more than they choose standard items directly off the menu, ensure your digital ordering interface makes "customizing an item" easy. Itsu, the UK Bento Box restaurant, does this particularly well. As the guest adds an item to their box, the item appears on the empty box on the screen—building the dish as you would in a brick-and-mortar fast-casual setup. This creates a great sense of theater and differentiation that can't be matched through a marketplace order.

Too many restaurants have settled for a standard copy of their dine-in menu with non-optimized photography and clunky PDF interfaces. Popmenu is addressing this challenge. CEO Brendan Sweeney says,

> Just a PDF, just a text representation of a menu is a terrible way to sell a restaurant. Menu is everything for restaurants. It is their most important, most impactful marketing tool. It shows everything: your creativity, your offering, the quality of your ingredients. And we just thought, 'Well, why is it represented in text?'

Tip: Count the clicks.

- Count the number of steps (or "clicks" of a mouse) to progress through your direct ordering channel as a registered user buying a standard order off the menu.

- Compare the number of steps to order that same basket off a third party's listing of your restaurant. For a non-customized item, it's likely to be 5 or 6 clicks.

- Amazon, with its "Buy It Now" button, is the gold standard (and therefore the consumer expectation) at 3 clicks.

- If your restaurant's ordering interface requires 8 or 9 clicks, think of that as 3 reasons why a customer will keep using the simpler, faster digital ordering interface of a marketplace.

Chipotle, in particular, is brilliant at digital ordering. They make it easy to order and especially easy to re-order. The "front pages" of leading digital restaurants' websites and apps are clean, uncluttered, and easy to navigate. Page loads are fast, and guests can quickly switch between adding an item and looking for another one. Customization is simple and built into the process. Add-ons and upsells are helpful—never annoying. They are typically part of the menu page or checkout page, rather than a pop-up or between-the-cart page that adds clicks and time to the process. They are typically dynamic—meaning they take into account what is already in the current cart and the order history of the guest—rather than offering a standard upsell or cross-sell that may be irrelevant to the context of the transaction. Gary Weyel of Bounteous, a digital experience consultancy, says, "Upselling and cross-selling can offer additional value to guests, but without appropriate context, retailers can also risk alienating them because the offers aren't relevant or engaging enough."[12]

Digital Payment

Getting payment right also means making it as frictionless as possible. Unless a guest orders from your restaurant with a level of extreme frequency that few achieve, most guests don't want to load their credit card information into your site.

While the US lags behind many other Western nations in their use of digital wallets[13], the US guest is fast becoming more expectant of frictionless payment solutions. In February of 2022, US guests spent $8.1 billion on restaurant purchases via digital wallets. That represented only 6 percent of sales whereas cash ($8.3 billion) accounted for 16 percent.[14] According to a study from PYMNTS, 30 percent[15] of guests aged 21-35 have utilized a digital wallet and that 44% of millennials that have not used a digital wallet would likely use it in the the next year if it were available[16]. Contactless cards (39 percent), money transfer apps such as Venmo and Paypal (45 percent), and paying by text (22 percent) are also gathering traction. The same survey does show that younger guests are most interested in these payment methods and that appetite for digital payment does wane as age increases—but this indicates the preference for digital payment methods is only heading one way—UP.

This means your digital ordering channels should accept Apple Pay, Samsung Pay, and Google Pay. According to Incisiv, only 9 percent of fast casual restaurants and 25 percent of all restaurants accept Apple Pay.[17] According to another study,[18] 69 percent of guests say it's extremely important to have mobile wallet solutions available in QSR/fast-casual restaurants where convenience and speed are paramount. The gap between consumer expectations and restaurant offerings shows that when it comes to payment solutions, the restaurant industry still has a way to go to achieve digital maturity.

The benefits go beyond just the ease for the guest. Enabling digital payments also reduces the burden of cash upon your operation and increases the chance of incremental purchases, while reducing the burden of chargebacks and fraudulent transactions. Apple Pay's authentication protocols can play a role in preventing chargebacks because the cardholder has to add the card to their mobile device, and authenticate the transaction each time through facial or touch ID. In this sense, it's what is called a "Container Wallet" since Apple doesn't store money—it just provides a container for the customer's payment credentials and allows a customer to purchase without revealing any personal data.

Again, the idea here is to make ordering as easy as possible. Insert the least amount of action between hunger and satiation. If checkout transactions are long, guests won't return or they will abandon a purchase altogether. You'd certainly notice if people got up and left your restaurant tables, so it's vitally important to monitor your e-commerce equivalent.

Loyalty

One out of three fast-food establishments and two out of three sit-down restaurants do not offer some form of reward program. Do loyalty programs provide unnecessary complexity to restaurants at an unnecessary cost? Clearly, the biggest chains don't think so. Starbucks provides free beverages or swag for earning their stars, and McDonalds offers free items to newly signed-up members. But can every restaurant afford to do this?

Loyalty programs come with three giant caveats. First, the main purpose of having a loyalty program is to know your guests—to acquire their information, track their behavior, and ultimately influence it. If your restaurant is not prepared to use the data a loyalty program collects, the cost of the program may not be worth it. Second, if your restaurant is able to acquire customer data through other means—a first-party ordering system, for example—loyalty may not be required. Third, it is crucial to monitor the points accrued. They can turn into a major liability for your restaurant if guests do not consistently redeem them.

Assuming your restaurant is prepared to use the acquired data, can't get the data any other way, and can manage points accrual, a loyalty program can be a great thing. In a survey carried out by Deloitte, out of 1000 guests, 79 percent said their participation in a program played a role in deciding where to dine.[19] So loyalty programs can help drive guest visits—and when executed effectively, they can drive higher check averages.

But in a digital world, loyalty programs can offer so much more than the type of loyalty programs used five years ago. Bringing the new loyalty capabilities into your digital strategy makes more sense now than ever before. Why? Because digitalization enables you to build a much greater appreciation of what drives your guests' actions and behavior, which in turn allows you to adapt your marketing very quickly towards results. Shaping a loyalty program from the ground up means you can skip the landline equivalent of the old "punch-based" loyalty cards that just gave away margin in the hope of improved guest frequency, and move to a far more powerful type of loyalty program.

Getting loyalty right means moving beyond discounts and punch cards to a system where restaurants use guest data to enhance the guest experience. Loyalty 3.0 enables personalization—in menus, offers, and experiences—in a way that enhances guest engagement with a brand. When a guest opts in to sharing their data with a brand, they expect that brand to use the data to make their life better.

Think of how personalized your Amazon experience is. Amazon isn't offering you a discount to order; rather, they are offering you a more relevant experience. This is the power that data makes available to restaurants. Zach Goldstein, founder and CEO of Thanx, a loyalty and personalization platform, says the move to first-party "is coming from a necessity to own the customer, but owning the customer is not really the end. It is a means to an action that is driving more revenue, driving more loyalty, driving more repeat purchasing from those customers. And that requires knowing who they are, giving them great channels to order digitally directly, and ultimately using the data that is captured through that process to personalize future interactions with customers so that you can build deeper data-driven relationships."[20]

Goldstein continues, "We're seeing a massive increase in the number of restaurants that are running loyalty. That's the good news. The bad news is that many are still treating loyalty programs like they start and stop at

Tip: Do loyalty right or not at all.

- Punch-card loyalty does not drive significant customer behavior, and it is expensive.
- The purpose of loyalty programs is to know your guest; use the data generated by the program to personalize each guest's experience.
- Gamification is more fun (and drives more behavior) than discounted products.

rewards." Goldstein believes personalization is critical for a loyalty program to have the desired business outcome a restaurant is looking for—incremental sales—and the desired brand engagement restaurants want. "If you're running what is actually a rewards program, not a loyalty program, you're not going to see much return on that. Loyalty is about driving lifetime value. It's about driving brand affinity. It's about driving referrals. It's about measuring satisfaction and engaging with it. And that's one of the things we focused on at Thanx —broadening the definition of loyalty to drive true personalization."

Sweetgreen announced in July 2022 that they are adding exclusive "gamification" offers to their direct channel, providing guests with more reasons to select their first-party channel over a third-party. Gamification is where an every-day activity, like going to a restaurant—becomes a game. This approach helps restaurants reward people for behaviors they want to encourage more of with things like badges, level-ups or VIP statuses. Chick-fil-A's program has three levels: each time a guest reaches a higher tier, they rack up more points, which converts to more enticing rewards. Starbucks' newly introduced "Odyssey" platform has embraced gamification too, with loyal guests able to take part in in-app games or challenges with the promise of receiving digital collectibles in the form of NFTs (non-fungible tokens) when they complete certain objectives or "journeys." Rewards are more than just free drinks. They're expected to be things such as free barista classes, or for the highest-performing guests, invites to international events.

There's a psychological aspect to gamification. Robert Cialdini's infamous principles of persuasion[21] such as scarcity—or as it's now widely known, FOMO (fear of missing out)—is a good example. Limited-time offers or specifically time-bound windows can drive fun and increased sales. Many guests will also share their status and rewards, increasing the chances of social media attention.

Fulfillment

Once the digital ordering experience has been perfected, a restaurant must get the food to the guest. This is what the third parties have made so easy for restaurants. The orders flow in, the food flows out. In a first-party order, getting the food out the door is now the responsibility of the restaurant.

Many restaurants have defaulted to driving customer pick-up as the easiest and least expensive way to fulfill an order. A substantial portion of guests engage in takeout, and making their journey easy is once again the main goal. Pick-up parking spots, directional signage and alphabetized shelves have become quite common. All of these elements will also help delivery drivers know where to go and improve order accuracy. Enabling quick pick-up is a core operational trait that should be considered at this stage of the digital maturity path to enable consistent quality of operation when further growth arises.

But what to do with the delivery orders that come through first-party interfaces? The DoorDash Drive product, the Olo Dispatch product, and the Toast TDS product all offer options to restaurants for fulfilling orders. DoorDash Drive makes the DoorDash delivery system—technology and drivers—available to restaurants whether the order comes in through their marketplace or through a restaurant's own website. Olo and Toast go one step further by matching restaurants up to different delivery options—DoorDash, Uber, Lyft, first-party delivery drivers, or a host of local delivery options, including those who are members of The RMDA (The Restaurant Marketing and Delivery Association, an organization of local delivery services). For restaurants that don't use one of these platforms, systems like Cartwheel and Shipday can match orders to delivery options.

Tip: Help drivers feel part of the team.

- A great driver experience is more likely to generate a great guest experience.
- Communicate through word and action that drivers who deliver from your restaurant will be treated well.
- Drivers drive to earn a living. The more meals they deliver, the more they earn—don't keep them waiting.
- Drivers are people: they appreciate warm greetings, free beverages, and samples.
- The better your restaurant treats drivers, the more likely drivers will remain in your restaurant's "red zone"—near enough to pick up your orders.

Conversion

Only after an amazing system has been set up—including great online ordering, easy payments, customized experiences based on the data guests are sharing with your restaurants, and low-cost/high-quality fulfillment—should you begin incentivizing guests to order direct through first-party interfaces. If the system isn't great, a guest may try first-party with your restaurant, but they won't come back. Make the experience great, then spend money getting guests to try it.

But even with a great experience, some guests will need more convincing. Ciancio says there are five tactics that will move guests over to first-party.

1. **Eliminate items on third-party.** Put the staples on third-party but restrict it. The greatest hits should only be on the first-party. McRib should only be on the first-party.

2. **Charge higher prices outside direct channels.** Make sure guests know that they "are going to pay more through the third-party than through the first-party.

3. **Use in-bag messaging.** Most people put in a QR code that offers an order with a discount. Start with feedback. Do you know what they are not thinking when they are sitting on their couch eating KFC? 'Let's order this again

Tip: Tell guests what you want them to do.

- Let guests know your restaurant offers first-party ordering.
- Message to guests' interests: many surveys reveal more than 50 percent of guests want to order direct to save on fees, have a better experience, and support their local restaurants.
- Use your existing assets to communicate: in-store, packaging, bag inserts, etc.
- Social media engagement should direct traffic towards your first-party platform.

in 5 minutes.' Get them into your CRM (Customer Relationship Management system) by asking for feedback.

4. **Brand the bag.** If I have an experience with your brand and it comes in a Grubhub bag, I didn't have an experience with your brand. I had an experience with Grubhub.

Invest in packaging. Mr. Beast Burger is a cool man. It shows up in a Beast Burger box and Beast Burger wrapper. They are taking the restaurant experience and putting it into the packaging. What if the happy meal came in a brown paper sack? That's not fun. People don't choose restaurants because they are hungry. They choose them because they are an experience or they are convenient. You can be both. And your packaging has to represent the brand. Whimsical? Environmental?

Conversion remains incredibly difficult; wresting customer attention from the marketplaces is an uphill battle. Today, the value through a marketplace and a first-party channel is inherently similar. If we examine other verticals—such as hotels—that are further along in this digitization journey, we see that they use direct ordering channels to provide value, conditioning certain consumer segments away from marketplaces. Finding ways to differentiate and give customers what they want and to offer it ONLY through first-party channels will likely forge the path that will drive more conversion in the years ahead.

SUMMARY: CONVERT FANS

- First-party ordering is not about turning your menu into a PDF file.

- The Capability Triangle shapes the basic requirements for a modern first-party ordering experience—digital ordering, payment, and loyalty.

- Count the clicks for a registered user to order a basic item from your menu. Compare it to the number of steps it takes for a guest using your main marketplace channel.

- Enabling easy payment (through digital wallet payments like Apple Pay or Google Pay) reduces friction.

- Digital loyalty programs offer your restaurant far more capability than traditional punch card mechanisms. Use loyalty as a differentiator to third-party marketplaces or don't use it at all.

- Consider your first-party fulfillment path. Will you use the easiest solution (Door-Dash, Toast, Olo) or forge your own path (in-house drivers, local delivery network)?

- Use multiple touchpoints across your entire restaurant to inform the guest of your first-How would you like to differentiate your first-party ordering experience from a third-party marketplace experience (packaging, user experience, quality, loyalty program, post-delivery experience)?

  # TIME FOR REFLECTION!

CHAPTER 2: CONVERT FANS

Download the app offered by any one or all of these companies onto your phone: Chipotle, Panera Bread, McDonald's, Chick-fil-A, Cava, Starbucks, Sweetgreen, Itsu, or Wingstop. Choose one that you've never used or registered with before.

If you don't have these restaurants near to you, choose a big brand that you respect that has clearly invested in a high-end first-party ordering channel.

1. With that app in mind, what do you like/dislike about the following and what would you incorporate into your own direct ordering channel?

	Like	Dislike	Incorporate into your own channel
Registration sign-up process			
Welcome email/text message			
Menu design and item descriptions/imagery			

Process to add items to the cart			
Payment setup			
If you can, order something from the app for delivery.			
Information provided to you post-transaction			
Packaging and information provided to you about the brand/first-party channels			
Overall impression			

2. What steps can you take to improve the relationship between your restaurant team and the drivers who take your food to customers?

3. Where in your restaurant can you tell your customers about your first-party ordering mobile site or app? How can you make it easy and enticing for customers to learn about it and use it?

4. How would you like to differentiate your first-party ordering experience from a third-party marketplace experience (pricing, products offered, packaging, user experience, quality, loyalty program, post-delivery experience)?

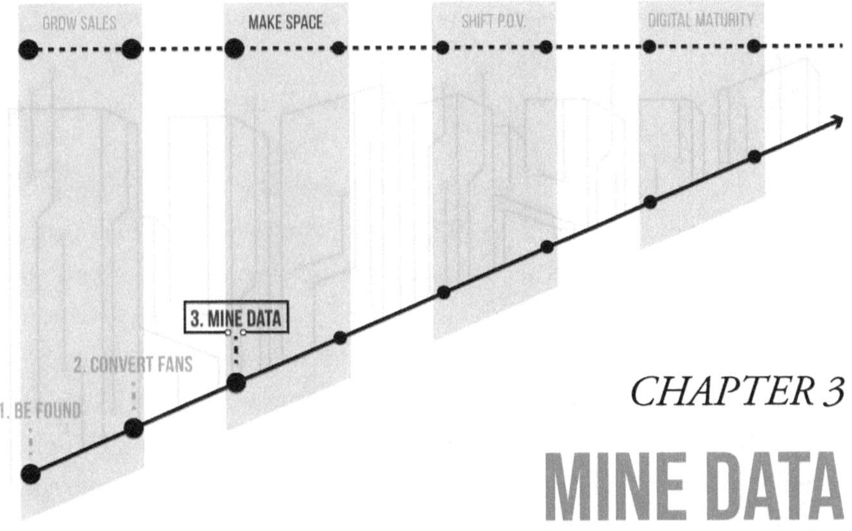

CHAPTER 3

MINE DATA

Walter peered over the starboard side of the boat. With a shuffle to the other side, he steered his attention back to his rod, which remained stationary. The morning air was still—much like his fishing rod. Nothing was biting. Across from Walter sat Felicia, his wife and fellow owner of their restaurant, Sydney's. Walter was the foody of the two of them, and Felicia was the brains. She did, among many other things, the books, the schedule, inventory management and payroll. She was finalizing the schedule for next week on her laptop while Walter fished. He looked over to her. "Done yet?" he asked.

"Yes—same as last week." she responded. Felicia rarely changed the schedule requirements but knew that within hours of putting it up on the board after printing out the Excel sheet, there would be the usual "Can I change this, can I change that?" from the team. It was frustrating her and had been for a while.

"You know, Walter, this laptop is like this lake."

Walter assumed the frigid air had slowed his comprehension as he replied in confusion, "You what?"

"The laptop." Felicia held it aloft. "It's got so much space on it—we'll call that the lake. And there are some good bits of information deep within my spreadsheets—we'll call them the fish. But what do we really do with it?"

"I have no idea what you're talking about," Walter grumbled, reeling in the line.

Sipping from her steaming cup of coffee, Felicia stood up, walked over to Walter, and sat beside him. "We need to know what we're looking for in these numbers. Be it the schedule, the accounts, or the reports we could download from the system. We don't just need the lake. We need a better fishing rod," she asserted. "If we know what we're looking for, we can use the information I pull together to make better decisions."

"Whatever you say, dear." Walter smirked. "She sure is the smart one out of the two of us," he thought, as he cast his rod out into the lake again—hoping for better luck on the other side.

In the old days of restaurants—as little as five years ago, in the 2010s—three reports could tell most operators how successful the prior period had been:

1. **The Sales report**, showing whether sales were up or down and whether price or transactions had been the reason.

2. **The P-mix report**, showing which items were selling and at what theoretical margin.

3. **The Hours report**, showing how much labor had been deployed to achieve the above.

"Taking these together," says Tony Smith, CEO of Restaurant365, "We get prime costs. The equation that everyone looks at is sales minus food costs minus labor costs, or prime costs. Somewhere in America, this report runs every 2 seconds," Smith says to depict how critical this information is for restaurants.[22] His company, Restaurant365, has historically been an accounting suite for restaurants but has expanded into many back-of-house functions through both acquisition (such as Compeat) and in-house building of additional features.

A beautiful, if not also somewhat overwhelming, thing occurred when new channels opened up and restaurant guests became known: sources of and detractors to profitability actually became less clear than they once were.

What had previously been hidden in averages of unknown detail could now be pulled apart to reveal surprising insights, but it takes work. "There are multiple channels out there. This is how much I'm moving in delivery vs. catering vs. takeout or drive-thru and on-premise. Within delivery, this is how much I'm moving by each delivery service," says Smith. "Then within that, you can look at products moving through each channel. Then, if you have the right digitization, you can understand the food costs of each item. That gives you the profitability by item by channel."

Are all channels equally profitable? It's hard to say without understanding how pricing differs, how partner charges differ, how food & paper (F&P) costs differ, and how labor differs. For example, one might be tempted to say that third-party sales are less profitable, focusing on the 20-something percent fee the platforms are charging coupled with takeout packaging and a lower beverage incidence. But let's imagine a scenario where the prices and the costs are so different from dine-in that third-party is actually more profitable. Imagine your restaurant has increased menu prices by 25 percent vs. a 20 percent third-party charge: already the profitability is close. Now imagine your restaurant requires servers and dishwashers for dine-in but no dedicated labor to place an off-premise order on a shelf for pickup. Suddenly, the third-party revenue is looking fairly attractive.

Taking Smith's logic even further, we can explore the question: are all guests equally profitable? Intuitively all restaurants know that some guests are deal-seekers, while others always add sides, desserts, and drinks. Before now, it was never clear exactly who was who at scale. Now, tracking purchases at the individual guest level enables a restaurant to focus on those who are most profitable.

And then the hard part comes: matrixing all this information together—products x channels x guests, where each may have different pricing, partner charges, F&P costs, and labor. If one could only see all this information clearly, one would know where to double down, where to deprioritize, where to make changes. To that end, Toast rolled out a new module in November 2021 aimed at helping restaurants understand profit by channel called the Performance Center.

In the manufacturing industry, companies take the detailed costing information, then overlay customer agreements on top of product-level

- Master menu management, a function that has historically resided in the POS for most restaurants, is the root of all subsequent data.

- Ensuring products are named clearly, assigned to appropriate categories, and have consistent and pre-determined modifiers will make later analysis much easier.

- Eliminate any one-off, manual adjustments (e.g., make your "half portion" option its own item in the menu rather than a manual note on an order).

economics to get a full picture of profitability. The exact same product may be more profitable when sold to, say, Walmart, than it is when sold to Costco due to pricing, shipping arrangements, promotional spend, chargeback allowances, and so on. The digitized restaurant creates the data that makes this level of detailed understanding possible for foodservice, in the same way manufacturing has been using data for many years.

A modern, digitized view of a restaurant's profitability is more nuanced than the averages, and requires the kinds of business intelligence analytics that were once used by only very large chains. The good news is that each software suite is working towards making the analytics repeatable and easy to use. The bad news is that with so many different systems in use by restaurants today, there is no single source of truth to answer the key questions that will move the needle on profitability. Let's take the industry's three most important reports, and see how digitization enables restaurants to dive deeper to get the insights that will move their businesses forward.

Sales Data: Using the e-Commerce Funnel to Increase Revenue

Restaurants are increasingly driving revenue through digital channels, and a powerful data stream has emerged: customer data. One restaurant CMO friend paraphrased mathematician Clive Humby, saying "Data is the new oil. It's valuable, plentiful, but unrefined it cannot really be used."

The playbook for today's restaurant marketer has dramatically shifted in focus and required capability. Historically, restaurants have somewhat blindly invested in three activities to increase revenue—awareness, trial, and repeat—where the goal of the first two activities is to expand reach among guests (greater percentage of nearby potential guests using the brand), and the goal of the last activity is to grow the frequency of those guests using the brand. Just 10 years ago, measuring the success of these efforts was incredibly challenging. Restaurants were blind, because they had no direct way of measuring who was aware, who had tried, and how often a guest came back. At best, restaurants were able to estimate levels based on consumer surveys not tied to individual guests.

Larger restaurant chains would estimate consumer sentiment, demographic makeup and buying behavior based on survey data or loyalty programs that covered at most 10 percent of their guests to determine the profiles of segments using their brand. These profiles would periodically get updated and shape marketing campaigns. Not every restaurant group, however, has a loyalty program, and even those that do don't always have the resources to dedicate to determining what the data says about their loyal base.

However, it's not necessary for every restaurant group to have a loyalty program—especially if your network is small or has fewer than 50 locations. As Abhinav Kapur of Bikky tells us, it's also about determining the amount of data you will realistically attain when considering the size of your restaurant business.

> Brands we work with typically serve 4,000 unique guests per location, per month. So at 20 locations, that's 80,000 guests per month. If we assume (generously) that 20 percent of guests opt into a loyalty program, that's 16,000 loyalty guests per month. Guest churn after first order in the restaurant industry (including loyalty) is 85 to 90 percent, so you're only acquiring 1,600 engaged loyalty users per month. That's only 2 percent of your monthly guests. Instead of allocating budget to maintaining and driving traffic to an underused app, what if that spend was allocated to activities that focus on net-new guest acquisition and data activation—without the marketing constraints of needing to drive app downloads?[23]

Tip: Collate your customer data—now.

- Your reservations data is a wealth of customer data. Collect it into one place and keep track of the source.

- Your social media followers and commenters provide customer / potential customer data. Collect it into the same place as noted above and keep track of the source.

- Your phone orders are another source of customer data. Record the name, address and telephone number into the same place as above and keep track of them as "phone orders."

- Ask yourself: Where else do you have customer data? Collect it now so that when you're ready to use it, you have your seed list ready.

Kapur makes a lot of sense in his guidance here because loyalty programs, app development and the necessary resources to maintain them can be incredibly draining upon smaller restaurant groups. But even without a loyalty program, that shouldn't preclude digital restaurant operators from exploring the value of guest data.

In an increasingly digitally-commerce driven world, every transaction (e.g., where the guest is known in some capacity by some identifier like a cell phone number, credit card, or email) has become trackable. And yet for many restaurateurs, the data that is available is not utilized as efficiently as it could be. With that inefficiency, a key thread of value that drives optimized profitability is lost. By moving away from averages and towards a system-atized view of guest data, most restaurants can easily track and influence the metrics that drive sales.

As restaurants become e-commerce companies, the "e-commerce funnel" can help them target the most impactful areas to increase revenue. The e-commerce funnel tracks specific consumer behavior as they move from viewing a restaurant, to accessing a restaurant's menu page, to viewing a product detail page (or item on the menu), to putting an item into the shopping basket, to attaching additional items, to checking out. The data can then be parsed further to differentiate between new and existing guests, an individual product's impact on rates of guests moving from one stage to the next, behavioral differences between platforms and compared to direct orders, and the impact of various offers.

DoorDash, UberEats, and Grubhub report data in a way that helps restaurants understand how their funnel is performing within each marketplace. As the platforms continue to innovate to introduce new dashboards and reports, it will become easier and easier for an individual restaurant to understand where its opportunities are. We would not be surprised if future versions shared average performance of restaurants on the platform, which will help individual restaurants detect where they are falling short and need to make an investment vs. where they are excelling and should continue to perform. The platforms might even highlight the most impactful areas to focus on, or recommend actions to improve each metric.

The easiest place to start using this data is within a platform. If the majority of your restaurant's online sales are on DoorDash, start with DoorDash. If your restaurant's sales are evenly split between sources, you may need to learn the interfaces of multiple platforms, download the data into Excel for comparison, or rely on software—like Toast's—to help make sense of the different data streams.

"Restaurants are continuing to diversify the way they reach customers

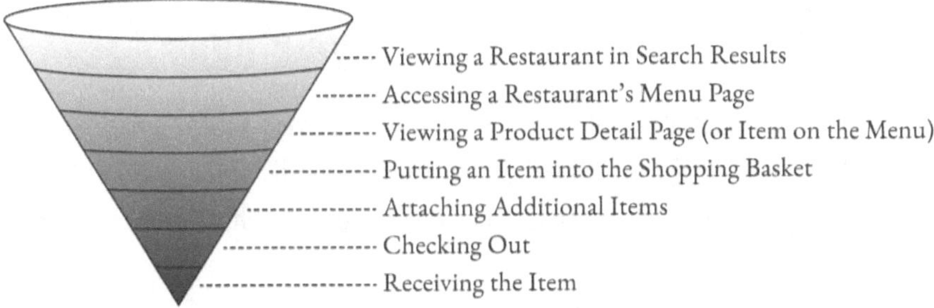

Figure 3.1 The e-Commerce Funnel

online. Whether that's through first-party or third-party channels, it's imperative that operators identify and analyze key metrics that affect their ability to grow digitally," says Ryan Parietti, Head of US Restaurants at DoorDash. "The Insights Hub within our Merchant Portal was built from feedback from partners, who emphasized that a breakdown of where their customers are located, what menu items are performing well and which could be removed, plus return on ad spend are crucial to their delivery optimization."

Google, as the ultimate search engine, has refined its analytics dashboard (now known as Google Business Profile Insights) to heights that even the biggest marketplaces and best first-party ordering providers are still working to match. Whether a consumer is finding your restaurant on the third-party platforms or via a Google search, the questions are the same. You must learn who your guests are, how they got to your digital storefront, what they do when they are there and how many of them take the actions you want (e.g., buy from you).

It is important to ask any first-party ordering provider (such as Olo, Toast, ChowNow, or Lunchbox) whether your menu on their platform is visible to Google Analytics. Some first-party ordering platforms keep the menu on their own website. When a guest clicks "order" on your restaurant's website, they "clickover" to the ordering platform's website. This can mean that Google analytics is not available to you, in which case you would need to get your ecommerce performance data from the first-party ordering platform you use.

Tip: Set up automated reports to show up in your inbox.

- Checking on Google's backend not your thing? Set up your favorite reports to be delivered straight to your inbox on the day you set aside to analyze your business.

- Many reports can be configured to match your preference: what matters most to you and how you like to see it.

- Reports are only as good as the actions you take from them. Ask yourself, "Knowing this, what, if anything, should I do differently?"

METRICS TO MEASURE

Traffic Sources: How do your guests find you and where are they coming from?

Traffic Sources reveal the percentage of recent visitors and how they arrived at your site. Are guests finding your restaurant when they search for items your restaurant offers and your restaurant's physical location? Are your paid Instagram ads driving traffic, or is organic search the driver? Google breaks results down by Direct, Paid Search, Unassigned, Organic Search, Organic Social, and Other Sources. This helps you determine how effective your marketing campaigns are, and where to continue spending. It also helps you determine where your content strategy or SEO efforts are succeeding or failing. Similarly, user location is provided to help restaurant owners learn if the traffic coming to their site is within a relevant trade area.

Bounce Rate: How many guests do not engage?

Bounce Rate is the metric that helps inform what percentage of guests arrive at your restaurant page and then leave without exploring any further—they're bouncing out, so to speak. Monitoring the number over time will help optimize particular pages and menu engineering efforts. Note that bounce rate can also be a factor of site loading times, so be sure to check your page load speed first. If your first-party channel and website takes a long time to open, those seconds can add "friction" to the guest experience and prompt them to try someone else.

Exit Page: Where do your guests leave you?

Using "Exit Page" metrics help you determine where customers leave you most often. Don't fret if the most common exit page is your home page; that is very common. You should take different corrective action depending on whether guests are leaving on the menu page, the item detail page, or the cart.

Average Session Duration: How long do guests spend exploring your digital menu?

Average Session Duration is another metric Google Analytics can provide that informs you of how much time guests spend on your website. For restaurants, helping the guest order quickly and efficiently is important. If too much time is spent on average, there may be challenges in the menu design, the ease of guest navigation, or some friction in completing an order.

Conversion Rate: How many website visitors result in a sale?

Conversion Rate is a metric of how many guests complete a purchase after they visit your restaurant's website. While most guests that visit in person will turn into a 100 percent conversion, the temptation to try somewhere else in an online environment is a mere few clicks away. Conversion rates can be surprisingly low online, but don't be disheartened. For e-commerce companies, the conversion rate can be as low as 2 percent, which means for every 100 visitors to the website, only 2 complete a purchase. There are a variety of reasons for this—guests may be just browsing, or something may be seriously wrong. Restaurant conversion rates tend to be higher because most guests on a restaurant website have a strong intent to eat, but the number can still be dishearteningly low to restaurants new to this metric. Again, measuring your number over time will help you isolate patterns and see where you may need to improve: website friction, online ratings, price, merchandising, time to deliver, etc.

According to DoorDash,[24] merchandising matters. Menus that include header images can generate up to 50 percent more monthly sales, and those with logos generate 23 percent more than menus lacking these basic branding elements. When it comes to menu item detail, menus with item photos saw an increase of up to 44 percent in monthly sales, and those with item descriptions earned up to 18 percent more in sales each month.

Cart Abandonment Rate: How many guests select an item from the menu, only to never complete their purchase?

Cart Abandonment Rate is a metric of how many guests fail to complete a purchase even after making it most of the way through the process. A high cart abandonment rate in the restaurant industry typically suggests total basket price shock or payment troubles. Again, because restaurant shoppers have such a high purchase intent (they are typically only on a restaurant's website because they want to eat), just browsing is less likely to be the cause of cart abandonment than in other types of e-commerce shopping.

Visitor Return Rate: How many guests return to purchase from you again?

The Visitor Return Rate is probably one of the most valuable metrics because it shows how loyal guests are to the overall experience. When a guest determines that all things considered—brand, product, price, website friction, fulfillment—the experience was a good one, they come back. A high Visitor Return Rate demonstrates that you have provided a good overall experience and remain a top-of-mind choice for guests.

Factors can go beyond search engine or platform analytics. Specifically, looking across different marketplaces, you can determine why some menu items are purchased more from one marketplace versus another. Is the photo, the description, or the price the same? Does the item sit in the same menu categorization or order as on the other marketplace? Do add-ons get utilized better on specific third party marketplaces versus your own direct channel?

RETURN ON AD SPEND (ROAS) = REVENUE GENERATED FROM CAMPAIGN / CAMPAIGN-SPECIFIC ADVERTISING SPEND

Figure 3.2 Return on Ad Spend

The data-driven e-commerce approach also lets restaurants more directly measure advertising effectiveness—driving, in particular, the very top of the funnel. The number of new and returning guests clicking into your restaurant's menu page is critical to ensure that what comes out of the bottom of the funnel is orders…lots of orders. E-commerce businesses use a concept called "ROAS" (return on ad spend) to determine which ads are most productive, and therefore where they ought to deploy more funds.

Tip: Test your ability to reach customers through different incentives.

- There are multiple ways to reach your customers: email, text, social media posts, paid social media ads and more.

- Through digital marketing, you can test which mediums (the method of communication) and which mechanics (the type of messaging) work best.

- The workflows to manage these tests can be complicated as the number of messages grow. Loyalty programs, email marketing programs, text programs can support tracking results and build on lessons already learned.

A good ROAS in the e-Commerce world can be as little as 4:1 (that is to say, $4 in revenue generated for every $1 in ad spend), but restaurants' lower margins require a higher benchmark. For a 20 percent profit margin restaurant to break even on ad spend, a 5:1 ROAS is required ($5 revenue @ 20 percent margin = $1 profit on $1 ad spend = breakeven). As a result, restaurants should seek close to 10:1 ROAS unless the purpose of the ad is to acquire new guests at breakeven or even a loss, then hope those guests will continue with the brand bringing profitability with future purchases.

ROAS is where A/B testing comes in. In our first book, we discussed the concept of A/B testing in Chapter 12: Attracting Customers Who "Get" You. A/B testing involves putting out different versions of ads, then measuring what happens. Next, roll out more ads that have higher ROAS, and fewer ads that have lower ROAS. Constant experimenting and doubling down on the higher ROAS ads will lead to more efficient ad spend. Platforms like DoorDash calculate the ROAS of paid advertising within the DoorDash marketplace for you—and report out the results of each campaign.

ROAS results are sometimes surprising. What a restaurant owner thinks guests might be looking for is not always what guests respond to. Restaurant marketing veteran Ellie Doty says,

> You can do tiny tests for no cost. Word changes in the copy. Tiny adjustments to the offer. Little changes like when the offer is being made. In full service restaurants, we thought that digital promotional activity around the time of day that people were making meal decisions, about an hour before mealtime, would get us more redemptions and frequency–for example sending dinner emails or notifications just before dinner. In reality, we needed to talk about family dinners at lunchtime, because that's when guests who look for offers were planning dinner.[25]

The most important aspect of A/B testing is to place many small bets. Unlike traditional restaurant advertising, where the marketing dollars are spent before the effectiveness of the campaign is known, A/B testing might allocate a tiny fraction of the overall budget towards any one campaign. Marketers will then double-down on the most effective campaigns, allocating a larger portion of the budget to proven marketing approaches.

Janet Monroe, President of Indianapolis-based ClusterTruck, says of this practice

> We are running hundreds of advertisements simultaneously on third party platforms and evaluating the performance of a variety of brands in multiple markets. What we are finding through this initiative is that the advertisements that simply help improve a brand's ranking within a platform don't necessarily work. You need more than just to be found. You need to give the consumer an incentive to choose you over every other restaurant listed right next to your own brand.

In other words, stopping just at search engine optimization (SEO) is not enough. Ads need to drive conversion. Doty counsels,

> The culture needs to empower an individual or small team to try some stuff. It costs almost nothing to try, so let someone try. If the owner or executive team gets involved, suddenly it's too easy to say no. These tests aren't about putting out the perfectly designed message. They are about putting out many messages, and finding out which one is perfect.

Product Data: Developing a Real-Time View of Recipe Costing

Historically in restaurants, cost-related information was stored in manual, disparate, and disconnected systems that made tying this data together nearly impossible. "We need to move to a unified system of truth. And it needs to stem from the recipe. If you structure a recipe properly, all the information you need is there," says Ian Christopher at Galley Solutions. Galley Solutions has created an inventory system with real-time costing data at the recipe level. "Ultimately we have a more resolved understanding of financial data."

As an example, if the cost of short ribs increases week to week, a restaurant can immediately see the impact on food costs at the menu-item level based on the volume of short ribs used in a dish. This enables the restaurant to substitute a lower-cost dish, increase the price of the short-rib dish, or choose to sacrifice margin as a loss-leader.

Should the restaurant choose to increase the price of the short-rib dish, it can now do so in a more nuanced way. Some restaurants are tempted to increase the price of a dish by the same amount as the increase of the main ingredient (short ribs are up 20 percent, so the menu item price should increase by 20 percent). Some restaurants recognize that although food costs are up, other costs may not be. As food costs are only 30 percent of the total P&L, these restaurants will instead increase the menu item price by 6 percent (20 percent*30 percent). With a solution like Galley, a restaurant could see that the short rib ingredient makes up only 15 percent of the total menu item price, and therefore increase prices by only 3 percent to make up for the short rib increase (20 percent*15 percent). Tightening up price increases in this way can avoid shocking guests into not coming back while still maintaining restaurant margins.

Restaurants who view themselves as manufacturers have a leg up in using all this data, according to Christopher. Manufacturers execute detailed cost accounting, allocating the bill of materials (BOM) with the latest inventory costs, machine times, and labor to specific product manufacturing runs to create product-level costing. Galley applies this same thinking to restaurants, enabling them to understand their profitability at a new level of detail that was not previously possible. Food costs are a great place to start, but software like Galley enables so much more.

Suddenly, instead of just seeing the food cost-of-sales for a given menu item, restaurants can see the complete cost, just like in a manufacturing plant. Not merely the latest inventory costs, but also station times and labor intensity. While the fried potatoes may have the lowest food cost, they may take up the most frier time. The fried chicken may have a lower food cost than other proteins, but it may also be the most labor-intensive. Viewing all three pieces of the puzzle together enable the restaurant to accurately understand item-level costs across the menu.

This is particularly important now: since the early 1980s, when inflation entered a 40-year low and stable period, restaurants have been able to focus just on food costs, which perhaps occasionally spike during a supply shock in a specific commodity—beef, for example. In the past, labor costs rose barely, if at all, and a smart restaurateur who managed labor scheduling on the whole could handle any changes. From handling the supply-chain shocks of the pandemic to the labor shortages resulting in an ongoing inflationary environment across all input costs—both food and labor—restaurants require the kind of comprehensive understanding that will enable them to protect margins without sacrificing guest traffic. According to Black Box Intelligence, in 2022, restaurants may have pushed past this mark. Pricing is up industry-wide between 5 and 10 percent in 2022 vs. 2021. Meanwhile, transactions have been down for 8 straight months, hitting a low point in July of 2022 of -6.8 percent. More surgical price increases, enabled by a more refined understanding of cost data, may better balance these two sales drivers.[26]

Hours Data

With a more refined grasp on sales data, the traditional idea of having a set required amount of labor hours to run the restaurant is being thrown out the window. X line cooks, Y servers, and Z front of house attendants for busy nights—while keeping a lighter schedule for your quieter day parts—is a blunt-instrument strategy compared to a restaurant harnessing historical data and AI-informed forecasts.

In the post-COVID era, we see workers not returning to restaurants, and throughout 2022, restaurants remained under-staffed. Workers are demanding better conditions—understandably requiring what would be offered in other (and, arguably, easier to work in) verticals. The restaurant labor crisis is not new. The restaurant industry has seen staff turnover far higher than the rest of the private sector for many years. In 2019, the overall hospitality industry had a turnover rate of 78.9 percent, according to the Bureau of Labor Statistics. During the first year of the pandemic, that rate soared to 130.7 percent, with fast food restaurants experiencing 144 percent in 2021. These numbers tell us that retention is perhaps more important than attraction—especially considering the $6,000 estimated cost to replace an existing employee.[27]

A top request from workers? Flexibility. In a recent 7Shifts survey of 3700 restaurant workers, 56 percent of them said more flexibility would "greatly affect" their happiness at work.[28] The modern restaurant worker wants to work on their terms and is more likely to be drawn to employers that address the importance of flexible schedules. While different employees define flexibility differently, most workers want their requests in scheduling to be consistently honored so that they can accommodate their other commitments—another job, school, family, or friends. These requests make workers less fungible, meaning it's harder to make a schedule because there are more constraints around who works which shift. These constraints, combined with an overall shortage of workers, make scheduling an arduous task.

Utilizing a labor scheduling software such as 7Shifts can simplify scheduling and communication with team members. Team members whose definition of flexibility includes last-minute changes can switch shifts without involving a manager. Restaurant owner Mike Bausch calls it "scheduling with empathy," and he believes offering the flexibility enabled by technology is a leading contributor to his industry-leading low employee turnover rates of just 35 percent annually.[29]

Scheduling software can build labor requirements based on the forecasted sales for a given day or time period. The manager can then spend time thinking through how to get new team members trained, or where more dedicated support might be needed (e.g., takeout is busy on Friday nights so an extra expo will be needed).

Restaurant labor software like 7Shifts makes it easy to apply the analysis that is occurring within the system. Rather than having to learn how to analyze all the data being created by digital operations, the modern restaurant operator can focus on using the insights. Whether it be with sales trends, product-level margins, or activity-based scheduling, the more restaurant technology offers insights and next steps, the better. Platforms like Wobot AI, which place cameras above stations and other areas of activity to measure repeatable processes, can identify deficiencies to defined processes. These technological, software-driven insights can shape improvements without the need for a group of consultants or supervisors with stopwatches. They can identify specific employees needing training or where best performers shine and in which areas. All of these insights can then lead to more enhanced schedules by placing the best employees in the best areas at the most appropriate times.

Transactions per labor hour or sales per labor hour is the best metric to use when tracking labor. Tracking it at the weekly, daily, and day-part level helps operators get out ahead of costly labor misallocations. Sophisticated operators may also look at on-premise vs. off-premise sales and catering vs. other off-premise sales, as these different types of revenue have different labor requirements.

The benefit of back-of-house scheduling and analytics software for restaurant owners? More tools are available to improve that metric through more informed decisions. Getting such information in real-time gives your restaurant the chance to change the outcome before it is recorded in the P&L. Once the books are closed, the outcome cannot be changed. The P&L is a lagging indicator. Metrics like transactions per labor hour are leading indicators—daily or weekly review of these numbers enable restaurateurs to make changes before the money has been spent. As an example of how powerful this data can be, Canadian bubble tea franchise Chatime used 7Shifts to get schedules out of spreadsheets and into the digital world. With real-time access to labor and sales data, they improved their labor percentage by 13 points—from 37 percent to 24 percent.[30]

Jordan Boesch, CEO of 7Shifts, describes the use of leading indicators this way:

> The way of the future is for restaurants to lean into data. There are
> so many old processes and systems still in use today that don't give

operators the information they need to plan ahead, then to adjust accordingly to make the best decisions in real-time. It's making schedules that pull in labor and sales data from one system to another so you can confidently forecast your needs, then balancing the employees' requested hours with your business needs. It's bringing a level of insight that allows you to make adjustments to labor through the day so you hit your targets regularly. It really is like adding a layer of confidence to the day to day of your business so you aren't looking back at the end of the month thinking, 'What happened here? Why is this number off? How did we miss labor targets?' The best decisions come from having the right data at the right time to plan, then react, and adapt in real-time if need be—that's where (the right) tech fills a gap.[31]

LTV-to-CAC: The Ultimate Yardstick

Taking all of this data together—an understanding of guest-level sales, guest-level marketing productivity, and specific, real-time menu-item costs, along with the labor required for different types of activity—restaurants can now generate the ultimate yardstick of performance. LTV:CAC (LifeTime Value : Customer Acquisition Cost, pronounced LTV-to-CAC) is a simple e-commerce concept that summarizes all the data into one metric.

CUSTOMER ACQUISITION COST (CAC) = MARKETING SPEND IN DOLLARS / NUMBER OF NEW GUESTS

Figure 3.3 Customer Acquisition Cost

In CAC (Customer Acquisition Cost), a restaurant calculates the cost to acquire a new customer. At the average level, this is all marketing spend divided by all new guests served during the same time period.

At a specific level, restaurants can assign marketing spend and number of new guests to specific campaigns. For example, a campaign that brought in more guests for fewer dollars (higher ROAS) has a lower customer

Tip: Calculate your average customer lifetime value.

- The formula: Lifespan of guest engagement in years (A) x Number of visits per year (B) x Spend per visit (C) x Restaurant margin (D).

- You should have a clear view of (C) and (D), but (A) and (B) can be more difficult to determine.

- To calculate the lifespan of guest engagement in years (A), assume one year at the beginning of the digital journey. Later, when your restaurant has a longer guest history, you can refine this assumption.

- For average number of visits per year (B), your restaurant can survey, estimate, or use collected data as it develops more digital relationships with guests.

acquisition cost than one that was less productive. As another example, a campaign that included a discount offer can include the discount value in the marketing cost to get a more accurate view of the cost incurred to drive customer action.

**LIFETIME VALUE (LTV) =
LIFESPAN OF GUEST ENGAGEMENT IN YEARS x NUMBER OF VISITS PER YEAR x
SPEND PER VISIT x RESTAURANT MARGIN**

Figure 3.4 Lifetime Value

In LTV (lifetime value), a restaurant calculates the profit a new guest brings to the restaurant over the course of the guest's engagement with the brand. At the average level, this is the typical lifespan of a guest, the typical spend across that lifespan, and the average margins on that spend. Because most restaurants are early in collecting guest data, it is best to assume a one-year engagement. As restaurants have guest data for longer periods of time, they can refine this assumption to multiple-year lifespans.

CEO of loyalty platform Paytronix, Andrew Robbins, recently presented his organization's research into lifetime value. Robbins believes a new loyalty customer has a 44 percent chance of returning and because of this, only has an average LTV of $94.[32] This, he says, is "incredibly low" given the length of time a customer gave to registering (or downloading an app) in the first place.

It is why maintaining a regular cadence of communication with a customer is crucial to stay top of mind with all customers, even those who have already indicated an interest in your restaurant. If you can get a customer to return four times, there's a 90 percent chance of them returning and their LTV then rises to $405.[33] That's an astounding difference. Paytronix supports its customers by tracing the LTV of each customer and understanding how their frequency rate changes based on the varying incentives that are sent their way. This approach can then improve marketing efficacy for each guest or guest segment.

Restaurants can divide their guests into segments such as frequency. You will have loyalists who use the brand regularly vs. occasionalists who show up every now and again. Or fans who stick with the brand for many years vs. trialers who may come in for a deal but never return. Restaurants can also segment guests by profitability: for example, guests who make large purchases or those who buy the highest margin items vs. those who buy few items, focusing only on the discounted items.

The most sophisticated digital restaurants know which kinds of guests they want, and what offers those guests respond to. They are able to attract and retain the best guests, without wasting marketing expense on guests they don't want in the system. They use data to inform decisions, armed with the knowledge that their spend is focused on the best return. When you establish consistent and effective utilization of marketing spend, deliver on your brand promise, and deploy labor appropriately to enhance the experience, sales will follow and the lifetime value of a customer will increase. At this stage, you then must address the next step of the maturity curve—how to handle the operational complexity from all these extra sales, which is what we'll cover next.

SUMMARY: MINE DATA

- Sales, P-Mix, and Hours represent the foundation of all restaurant analysis and digitization enhances their capability.

- Profitability by channel differs; understand the costs, product mix, and pricing of each channel to determine channel-specific margins.

- Use platform and search engine analytics data to learn about your who your customers are, how you acquired them, how they behave when present on your digital assets, and how many convert into purchasing from you.

- Restaurants should seek close to 10:1 return on ad spend unless the purpose of the ad is to acquire new guests at breakeven.

- Structuring your recipes correctly will help you manage the data to track actual vs. theoretical costs.

- Using smart scheduling software increases labor efficiency, saves management time, and improves employee experience.

- LTV:CAC is the metric that digitally mature restaurants measure themselves on to ensure marketing spend is driving growth.

  **TIME FOR REFLECTION!**

CHAPTER 3: MINE DATA

1. Which metrics do you regularly analyze? Based on what you've read in this chapter, which metrics do you think are most appropriate for you to start measuring?

2. Find your conversion rate from each of the marketplaces you use today and your first-party platform. Notice how they differ from one another.

3. How do most guests find your restaurant's website? Check your Google Analytics dashboard. If you don't have it set up, do so, then come back to this question after your dashboard has been active for a month.

4. Find the ROAS from your last marketing campaign on your primary marketplace. What was the objective of that marketing campaign? If it was to drive profitable sales, the ROAS should be at least 5:1. If it was to acquire new customers that would later repeat at full price, the ROAS might be lower.

5. On a scale of 1 to 10 (10 being amazing), how structured and detailed are your menu recipe cards? Do you have a detailed breakdown of how much of each ingredient goes into each dish? If you scored yourself less than 5, what can you do to improve?

6. For the next month spend on marketing guest acquisition efforts, track how much is spent (A). Also track how many "new" guests have you served during the month (B). (Note—you may need to be more focused than usual on how you measure this if you don't have a system in pace.) Divide A by B to get your Customer Acquisition Cost.

7. What is the average number of times in a year that a guest uses your restaurant, including those who never return (A)? What is their average check size (B)? What is your typical restaurant margin (C)? Multiple AxBxC to get an average lifetime value within a year. Segment your customers by different metrics (channel, product, daypart) to compare LTVs.

8. What percentage of marketplace revenue have you spent on advertising each month for the last 6 months? DoorDash, by way of example, believes average promotional sales can grow by up to 20 percent and see a 5-6x ROAS (return on advertising spend). Calculate this for your restaurant and determine whether your restaurant sees this level of return.

	Ad spend $ (promotional placements & discounts offered)	Absolute sales attributed to ad campaign	ROAS = sales / advertising spend
Last month			
Two months ago			
Three months ago			
Four months ago			
Five months ago			
Six months ago			

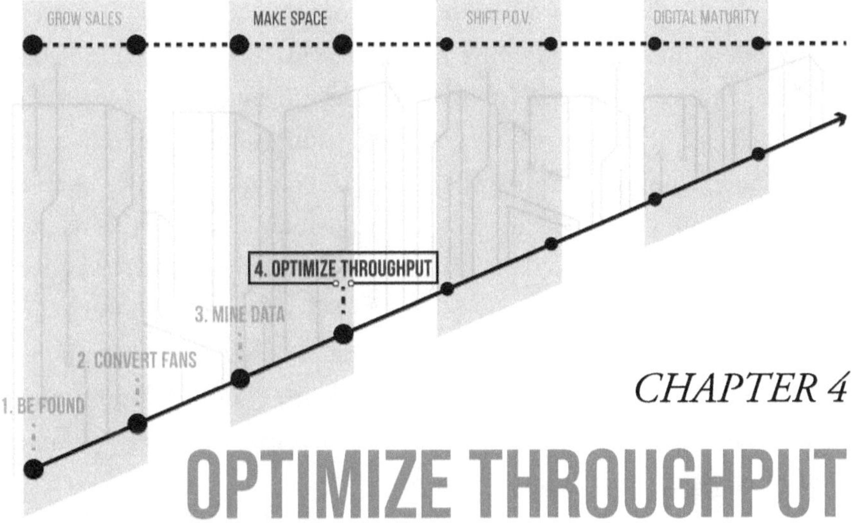

CHAPTER 4

OPTIMIZE THROUGHPUT

"That's tonight?!" exclaimed Carol.

Carol was flustered. Her husband Dave had invited their friends, Darius and Shanelle Clemson, over for dinner that night—which happened to be the same night she had arranged a similar dinner party for Marco and Dev! They hadn't even planned the meal, and now they had to cater for double the amount of guests. Darius and Shannelle had put on the most perfect dinner party a month prior, and on the way home, Carol had said to Dave, "Did you see how they managed that whole thing? Everything was so calm, and they each knew what the other was doing throughout."

"Tonight is not going to be calm," she thought as she frantically considered what to do.

"Let's just get in that gal who helped our neighbors to help us prep," suggested Dave.

"No way. That's not how we're going to do this thing. If the Clemsons don't need help, neither do we," Carol retorted.

Some hours later, both Carol and Dave had donned aprons, and Darius and Shanelle stood by the island, sampling their first glass of wine. The doorbell rang, and Marco with Dev held a bunch of flowers and a bottle of wine towards their host's front door. Shannelle answered the door as the situation in the kitchen was starting to unfold. Dave zigzagged behind Carol, and Carol did the same behind Dave. One went to the fridge, while the other went to the pantry, and as they returned, they almost bumped into each other in the middle. "Dave!" shouted Carol, so infuriated that the bowl of vegetables almost fell from her hands in between them. "Sorry," Dave said humbly with an awkward smirk towards the four guests observing. "What do you want me to do next?" he asked as they decided which of them was doing what with the bowl of vegetables in Carol's hands. The twisting, turning, and grumbling continued while their guests tried to converse politely without disrupting the chaos in front of them.

Driving home later, Darius reflected to his wife. "I don't think they really had a system of working. If they did, they'd have been able to put that on for another 6 guests without breaking a sweat."

"That's for sure," laughed Shannelle as she remembered her Grandma's wise words that she had shared with Darius ahead of their first dinner party some years earlier: "Know your role, know your station."

Stations + Roles = Capacity

Once a restaurant's third-party and direct channels are optimized, a new and somewhat welcome problem emerges: the restaurant begins to take on more orders than it can keep up with. So many new channels are opening up, and orders come in from everywhere. The first 10 percent increase feels great. The next 10 percent increase feels difficult but doable. Beyond that? Trouble.

Most kitchens are designed to handle the expected demand from the front-of-house. The number of tables and the turn time of those tables dictate the likely maximum number of dishes the kitchen must produce on any given evening. For example, if your restaurant has 30 tables, and the average turn time of those tables is an hour, and your dinner service lasts from 6 p.m. to 10 p.m., you'll have a maximum of 120 tables to service that evening. If the table serves an average of 6 dishes per table, that's a maximum of 720 dishes being served that evening.

Tip: Understand your theoretical maximum number of dishes per period.

- Determine how many tables your restaurant has. (A)

- Measure the number of minutes it takes from seating to exit for your average guest during peak period. Use a stopwatch, or watch previously recorded camera footage. (B)

- Note your busy rush time—e.g., an evening rush may last 4 hours, from 5:30 to 9:30 pm. (C)

- Using the reports from your POS, calculate the average number of items per table. (D)

- Multiply (A) by (B) by (C) by (D) to get your maximum dishes per peak period.

Of course, it's improbable that every table is full for the entire 4 hours of service, but it is these kinds of calculations that drive the design and staffing of the kitchen. The same is true for drive-thru restaurants; only in those cases, in addition to the table turns, restaurants must calculate the number of cars that can go through the drive-thru in an hour and the typical order from each car. The best restaurant managers consider past performance to forecast the necessary ingredients to schedule and the size of the team required to produce the dishes. The best restaurant designers will ensure the team has the optimal equipment to create those dishes quickly. However, the forecast falls short when third-party orders are layered on top.

First, most kitchens were not designed to handle an incremental 10 to 40 percent increase in transactions compared to what the dine-in or drive-thru can handle. Many years before delivery was imagined, the solution to this increase would have been to over-build a kitchen, wasting precious capital during construction.

Second, the factors that affect a restaurant's on-premise sales may differ from those that affect its off-premise sales. For example, two operators of the popular virtual brand Mr. Beast Burger said it was impossible to anticipate the level of demand. A surge of delivery orders would occur seemingly at random, but then the more observant operator noticed these surges tended to come within hours of Mr. Beast posting a new viral video on YouTube. Similarly, the weather can play a role. For example, if a snowstorm sweeps a particular area, the restaurant's on-premise sales may be quieter than usual, but delivery orders may rise.

Third, digital orders have no queue, no table reservation process, no full parking lot. There is no way for a digital consumer to determine that a particular restaurant is overwhelmed.

When first-party orders are added to the sales mix, there will likely be even more orders picked up by drivers or customers during peak windows of demand. A customer is a customer regardless of channel. By understanding volume across all sales channels, you can better accommodate your requirements for staffing—both in the kitchen but also for expo and front-of-house needs. Some restaurants consider having a dedicated person managing off-premise collections, to prevent the interruption of dine-in guests. Chipotle has created Chipotlanes, to enable the customer to use the drive-thru lanes (where provided) to collect without ever having to leave their cars, whereas McDonald's enables guests to choose how they wish to

Tip: Understand your sales mix by channel.

- Download a report from your POS for each month of the year at a transactional level.

- Total the sales for each channel you've received orders from (on-prem, delivery, pick-up, drive-thru, catering, etc.) by hour, day, and month.

- Observe unusual changes in channel performance.

- What drives unexpected peaks of sales to different channels? Do you notice any patterns such as weather, sporting events, or holidays?

collect an item (curbside pickup, drive-thru or inside the restaurant). This means the orders need a clear expo-instruction so that your expeditors easily know what to do with the item.

Throttling Is Not the Solution

The marketplaces and technology providers that enable online food delivery have tried to tackle the issue of sales when at capacity with throttling features. Throttling turns off or limits digital food delivery orders. During peak demand times, restaurant staff can choose to turn off digital channels to focus on the customers in front of them. Many restaurants actually encourage this behavior by training a customer service hierarchy. If you get busy, the thinking goes, turn off the lowest-margin channels first: perhaps the third-party marketplace your restaurant does not have a preferred agreement with, then the other third parties. If things get really bad, some go as

Tip: Know when to throttle—and when not to.

- From the sales mix report, filter out everything but your digital channels (such as a third-party marketplace).

- Find all the instances when you've only had one order or less in a particular hour.

- Count the frequency of low orders for that channel.

- Where you see frequent periods of 1 or fewer orders during periods that are typically busy, you may have a throttling problem.

- Many third-party platforms include a "percent uptime" metric in their merchant portal, which will tell you automatically what percent of the time your restaurant is online, and what percent it is offline (most likely due to throttling).

- Speak with your team and ask why they turn off digital channels and what parameters they use to determine when to turn them back on.

- Address process errors in retraining and ask yourself what can be done to avoid throttling even in the busiest periods. It is a sign that more support is needed.

far as to turn off the first-party channel and let the restaurant focus on guests walking in the door.

While this hierarchy sounds reasonable, it is a blunt instrument to address the challenge of insufficient peak-demand capacity. Throttling gives the off-premise guest an inconsistent experience of your restaurant. Imagine if you shut your physical doors occasionally at 7 p.m. on Friday nights because you got too busy. It would be ludicrous to do such a thing. Your restaurant team has been trained to handle busy occasions by suggesting the length of wait time the guest may have, inviting them to the bar for a drink during their wait, or by handing them menus to peruse. Turning off your digital channels is the equivalent of saying your restaurant is closed, with no indication of when it may reopen. The chance for acquiring a new customer is lost, and for loyal customers, you have potentially created a reason for them to try an alternative.

The second challenge with throttling is that employees can get so busy that they forget to turn the digital channels back on. Even without meaning to, a well-intentioned employee, following the customer service training, might get so distracted by dinner prep that they simply forget to switch back on the third-party channels, once again causing a potential loss of new customers or motivating old customers to look elsewhere.

Still not convinced throttling is bad for your restaurant? Turning off your restaurant's digital storefront, even for 15 minutes once a week, can train the algorithms to work unproductively for your business. Most obviously, if your restaurant isn't there, it isn't getting clicks or orders. The lack of this positive consumer feedback tells those algorithms that your restaurant isn't as popular as a restaurant that is open and getting clicks. Algorithms are impersonal. They don't care why something is happening, only that something is (or is not) happening.

With throttling, then, being clearly an unattractive way to deal with the problem of "too many sales," what is a restaurant to do? To address this challenge, three core actions must be taken first:

1. Identify the actual throughput capacity of your kitchen.
2. Understand what is required to increase it.
3. Develop a forecasting competence to adjust to anticipated surges.

Brian Reece and Steve Crowley co-founded the restaurant optimization organization Service Physics. They tackle challenges such as high transaction growth for restaurants, retailers, and other businesses requiring process capacity. Crowley says, "One question we get a lot is, 'What is the theoretical capacity of our kitchen?'" Their response always comes back to numbers. "There are 1,800 seconds in 30 minutes. It's reliable. It always has been and always will be, and it provides a bite-size way to think practically about your operation."[34]

Here's how Service Physics would approach the capacity challenge. If you time how quickly your operation can produce one order—called your "production pace"—you can calculate the capacity of your kitchen in a given 30-minute period using simple division.

Example: 30-minute production capacity

- 45 seconds to make a beverage: 1,800/45 = 40 beverages per 30 minutes.

- 40 seconds to fry an egg—with four burners, you can make one every 10 seconds: 1,800/10 = 180 eggs per 30 minutes.

- 60 seconds to bag a to-go order: 1,800/60 = 30 orders bagged per 30 minutes

Crowley says,

> In our experience, the limit is likely to be an inefficient work system that misapplies labor and underutilizes machines, rather than a maxed-out person or piece of equipment. Adding more people or machines may increase production, but at what incremental cost? It would be nice to increase production without adding any incremental cost.

This seems counterintuitive—and indeed, many operators' first response to capacity constraints is to add equipment or labor. But Service Physics studies equipment utilization in some of the country's busiest kitchens and more often finds that the very pieces of equipment operators want to add (e.g., another fryer) are only in full use about 50 percent of the time, even during the busiest rushes. In other words, there are peaks and valleys of equipment utilization. By smoothing out production to "continuous flow" (more on this later) these perceived equipment capacity constraints disappear.

Let's continue with the "1,800 seconds in 30 minutes" metric, but now we'll use it to determine your kitchen's throughput capacity.

Example Scenario:

- There are 40 customers currently dining in the restaurant.
- The restaurant has set an online order throttle at 10 orders per 30 minutes and receives all 10 of those orders.
- Let's assume 10 additional customers are trying to place orders online but are unable due to the throttling.
- Therefore, when we consider the orders across all channels, we have a demand of 60 total orders for the restaurant to potentially fulfill. The calculated customer demand rate is: 1,800/60 = 30 seconds (one order every 30 seconds).
- Currently, the hypothetical restaurant is only set up to capture 50 orders per 30 minutes due to the self-imposed limit on customer demand through throttling: 1,800/50 = 36 seconds (one order every 36 seconds).

In this example, six seconds per order is the gap for this restaurant's ability to increase sales by 20 percent (capturing those 10 throttled online orders). Throttling is easier than solving this capacity optimization challenge, right? Right—it is. But taking the easy route leaves a 20 percent revenue increase on the table and creates a poor experience for your unserved off-premise guests. And don't forget, you'll never hear about those off-premise guests because you never knew they were at your virtual front door wanting to order.

Still not convinced? Let's put some additional numbers into this example.

Example Opportunity: What is 1 second of optimized productivity worth to this restaurant?

- Let's assume this same restaurant has an average check of $20.

- Those 10 throttled online orders @ $20 each = $200 of peak half-hour opportunity from unmet demand.

- If we assume 10 hours of peak demand per week (or 20 peak 30-minute periods), the annual opportunity is: $200 unmet demand x 20 peak half-hours per week = $4,000 per week x 52 weeks/yr = $208,000 annually.

- Therefore, every second of production rate improvement we create is worth $34,666 ($208,000/6 seconds)

Crowley believes that optimized productivity doesn't require a massive investment, if any. Instead, he believes studious observation, testing, and realignment of the work can uncover opportunities.

> We have not yet seen a case where this kind of improvement required investing in equipment or labor. There is almost always plenty of opportunity just by studying how we work and steadily making improvements. The exception to the rule might be an urban environment with an extremely high peak 30-minute demand across both online and in-store channels.

Companies like Service Physics certainly can help restaurants, but their principles are derived from Kaizen and lean manufacturing, both of which are more commonly associated with factories making Hondas than kitchens making burritos. Although lean retail has been around for years—for example, Carl applied that principle at bp convenience stores—it's a relatively new approach in restaurants. The main opportunity here is to observe a kitchen with new eyes and believe it to be capable of more than it currently achieves. Reece and Crowley offer up their three favorite approaches to finding those spare seconds that will open up new capacity to service more orders—regardless of the channel.

The Mise-en-place Principle

Mise-en-place is the organized setup of a kitchen station, including the ingredients and equipment needed for the rush. When everything is in its place within an arm's length, a line cook working the station can produce any ordered meal without moving from the station. Anthony Bourdain explains mise-en-place in his book Kitchen Confidential with this story:

> I worked with a chef who used to step behind the line to a dirty cook's station in the middle of the rush to explain why the offending cook was falling behind. He'd press his palm down on the cutting board, which was littered with peppercorns, spattered sauce, bits of parsley, breadcrumbs, and the usual flotsam and jetsam that accumulates quickly on a station if not constantly wiped away with a moist side-towel. "You see this," he'd inquire, raising his palm so that the cook could see the bits of dirt and scraps sticking to his chef's palm, "That's what the inside of your head looks like now. Work clean!"

The Japanese equivalent of this, in "lean" language, is "5 S," which stands for the following:

1. **Seiri**—Sort items to retain, return, and rid
2. **Seiton**—Organize items in the workplace
3. **Seiso**—Clean the workplace
4. **Seiketsu**—Maintain Seiri, Seiton, and Seiso
5. **Shitsuke**—Discipline the organization

Understanding the steps of a sole cook in the production of items on your menu in a kitchen and how easily and efficiently that cook can perform their role without having to step out (as Bourdain puts it) of "arm's reach" is a quick way of identifying whether there are seconds to save in your kitchen. Similarly, how cleaning and replenishment are handled during service (and not just at the beginning or end) are easy visual cues that can help you determine whether a kitchen is becoming overburdened and where opportunities may arise. In Chapter 11 "Operating in a Virtual World" of our first book *Delivering the Digital Restaurant*, Reece and Crowley recommend the spaghetti diagram as a way of visually depicting how often a particular role is required to step out of their way to complete a task.

Reduce Shared Work & Simplify Tasks to Repeatable Routine Activities

Crowley believes shared work can also create an environment of "shirked accountability" and, as he says, "When everyone is responsible, no one is." Even if every worker has the best of intentions, it's easy during a rush to assume that someone else is on it. Service Physics has repeatedly demonstrated that workers with shared accountabilities walk more during a shift and are more easily distracted. Clearly defined roles and responsibilities for each workstation keep workers focused on the task at hand and ensure that one person is accountable for each task. In a labor-challenged environment, it's common to cross-train your restaurant workers so they can perform numerous tasks to support the wider team. We are not advocating against this, but we believe that for each role and workstation worked, the team member must know their required duties while stationed to that particular responsibility and stick to them.

Some readers may feel that setting roles in a kitchen is counterintuitive as bottlenecks could form, and kitchen managers could utilize dormant or inactive resources to eradicate challenges further up or down the line. In these instances, it's worth studying the entirety of the line and whether the steps are in the appropriate order and tasks have been allocated correctly.

Rearranging Equipment or Work Steps into a Continuous Flow

Eliyahu M. Goldratt says in his book, The Goal: A Process of Ongoing Improvement, "Since the strength of the chain is determined by the weakest link, then the first step to improve an organization must be to identify the weakest link." Identifying a restaurant's workflow chain and its weakest link begins by observing where items in the process build up, waiting for activation into the next stage of the process. Imagine a completed burger, fully garnished, packaged, and ready to go, but the fries aren't ready because the potatoes are still being peeled. In today's kitchen, where plating a burger and fries and "bagging" a burger and fries is two separate tasks, these types of delays can happen more often than we genuinely recognize.

However, this doesn't often happen in an In & Out restaurant where you see someone with a dedicated role, regularly using a specific piece of equipment to cut the potatoes. Likewise, it doesn't often happen in a McDonald's restaurant, where the fries are prepared in advance, in bulk at a commissary by equipment that prepares millions of pre-cooked fries before flash-freezing them and sending them to the restaurant. After cooking, french fries are staged in a "warm" zone beside the fryer for accessible collection after the burger flies down the chute for packing. These processes are so well-known to us as consumers that we are surprised and annoyed if fries are not immediately available in one of these establishments.

The steps a bag of french fries goes through to be seamlessly ready when other items are complete is an excellent example of a continuous flow of activity and how equipment should be used and positioned in a process.

The french fryer in most McDonald's is located on the left (if facing the kitchen), two steps from the chute, where the activity in the kitchen delivers the sandwiches. The french fry cutter in an In & Out is positioned above the water sink, ready for rinsing. The spinner, located to the side of the sink, removes excess water for 25 seconds. Then the uncooked fries are placed in a bowl, ready to be cooked in the fryer just behind them on the hot wall. Each piece of equipment is carefully placed adjacent to its immediate prior and next step.

It is also rare to see the equipment in these restaurants inactive—they are always "on." This is another way to identify opportunities to optimize your restaurant's equipment stack. If there are times when equipment is not fully utilized, ask yourself if that bottleneck could be the weakest link in your production.

It all seems rather obvious when you think about it, but decades of efficiency-driven focus has optimized the kitchen layout for these two incredible brands. Further still, they are optimized to accommodate both on- and off-premise channels to handle the tremendous volume and multiple ordering methods prevalent across most QSR brands today.

Tip: Optimize your logistics options.

- You don't need to rely on just third-party marketplace logistics fleets.
- Utilizing other logistics fleets enables you to improve the speed of delivery fulfillment.
- Pending your sales profiles, SaaS software can recommend which fleets to prioritize over others at specific times.

When to Turn to Technology to Increase Capacity

Many restaurants are hearing daily about robots, drones, and other forms of automation claiming to save material points on the labor line. What the most engineered QSR brands show the industry is that basic changes in the order of equipment on the line, the placement of people, and the routines the team is trained on can dramatically improve efficiency, and deliver the same results that automation promises, but without the upfront cost of purchasing a robot.

There are also ways to "automate" without going full robot. Consumer self-ordering via tablet, kiosk, mobile, or voice effectively automates the ordering process. Programmable ovens effectively automate cooking. Just as online reservation systems made hosts more effective with the guests in front of them because they were no longer on the phone, these small automations can improve the productivity of workers rather than outright replacing them.

For those restaurants who find their kitchens optimized and capable of tremendous throughput, the bottleneck for serving delivery moves to the logistics network between kitchen and consumer. The most convenient thing about third-party marketplaces is that they also provide delivery logistics. Restaurants who have built up a substantial first-party business have the option to use DoorDash, Uber, or Lift through products like DoorDash Drive ("Offer delivery from your own app or website by tapping into Door-

Dash's network of Dashers"), yet they may find they do not want to be tied to just one system. Perhaps they have discovered that their costs are lower when they use their own drivers at most times, but at others, they want to use a third-party. Perhaps they have found that different platforms are more effective at different times of the day.

If your restaurant is in this position, it can fulfill delivery orders with the flexibility of outside delivery providers by using a system like Shipday. Moin Islam, co-founder of Shipday, points out that in the food industry, "The industry embedded delivery inside the app—but we don't have to. Maybe at the beginning when there wasn't much demand, that was okay, but now it's time to separate these things out." By using specialists for each function (the order and the fulfillment), restaurants can save money on the guest acquisition, increase their data collection, and reduce the cost of delivery. Islam continues,

> We don't think you have to pay a commission for a delivery service. [Shipday] is a fulfillment platform. It is a commission-free delivery platform that manages delivery for you. It manages the delivery, not the fleet. We can automatically schedule which fulfillment partner gets what order—by distance, time, and cost. Then, there's real-time orchestration happening. We send an SMS with a live tracking link that has the same kind of tracking that a consumer would have with DoorDash.[35]

Islam sees restaurants becoming e-commerce companies, and their online orders as an e-commerce fulfillment challenge to solve.

> It's fast-moving, high-paced, high-velocity, but the fundamentals are the same. Anyone doing high volume starts doing self-delivery. It doesn't have to be either/or. It's a continuum. Optimize across whoever is available. Shippo or ShipStation do similar in e-commerce. But food is much more live—you need a decision in real-time. The probability of finding a driver is higher across multiple platforms, and you can find the best deals.

SUMMARY: OPTIMIZE THROUGHPUT

- Understand your maximum capacity in comparison to your current sales throughput.

- Learn what drives peaks in sales by channel, by month of the year, by day of the week, and by hour of the day to identify opportunities.

- Throttling can be effective and easier than addressing process inefficiencies, but it is likely not the best approach to tackle capacity challenges and will likely inhibit discovery on marketplaces.

- Once you determine your production pace, adding more employees and equipment will not always improve it.

- Set up workstations to minimize steps away from them.

- Identify which shared responsibilities are essential and which ones would be better serviced by just one person.

- Delivery logistics can be optimized by using more than just third-party marketplace logistics fleets. At certain times, certain driver pools are more numerate and available.

  **TIME FOR REFLECTION!**

CHAPTER 4: OPTIMIZE THROUGHPUT

1. Do you believe you have a capacity challenge at your restaurant? How would you describe the challenge? How would your team describe it?

2. When is your team most stretched? Which part of your team is stretched? Is this because of available staffing, or due to the amount of orders?

3. Work with your cooks to look at their workspace (think 5S). Is everything as organized as it could possibly be? What cleaning practices can be modified to improve cleanliness, but also ensure everything has a clear and obvious home when not in use?

4. Sketch out the process for making one of your most popular menu items. Measure the time it takes for that item to be completed through each step. For the lengthier steps, is the time taken because of the location of the work, the process itself, or something else? Consider which part of the process is the weakest link and what could be done to eliminate that element, or move it earlier in the workflow to prevent bottlenecks.

5. Sketch out a bird's eye view of your kitchen layout in the space below. Find a place where you can observe the team without getting in the way. Ask the team to go about their business as normal and do nothing different than usual. Consider which role in the kitchen has the most likely chance of distraction. For 30 minutes, hold a pencil to that worker's location and don't lift the pencil as they move around the kitchen. This will create what's called a spaghetti diagram as you draw their movements around the kitchen.

6. Review your spaghetti diagram. The points at which the individual had to move many times to the same location outside their immediate workspace is where an opportunity likely lies to improve the process of what the individual is doing or the location in which that individual is doing it. What other observations did you make? Where can you improve the workspace or workflow?

7. Now spend 30 minutes during a busy sales period in the week counting the number of footsteps per transaction taken. Also count the number of times the expo left their station and went to the pick-up area. How many journeys were made during those 30 minutes? How many steps per journey? What efficiencies could be made by addressing the expo station location or the pick-up area location?

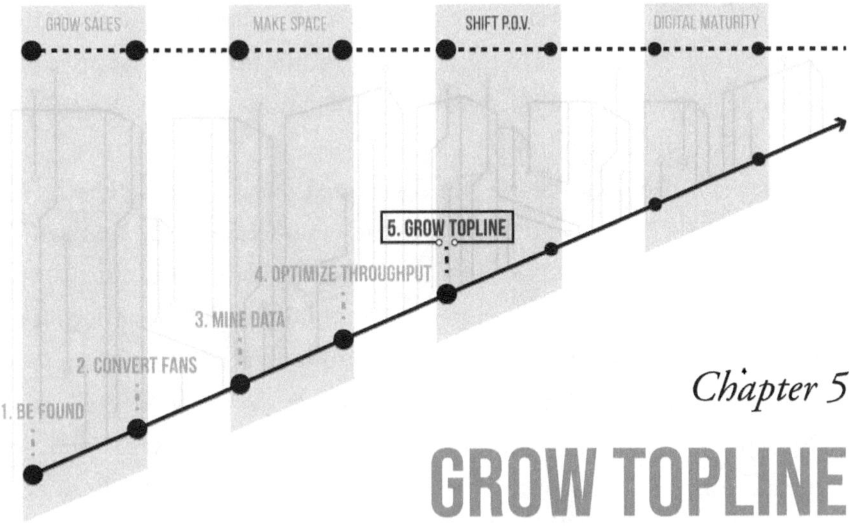

Chapter 5

GROW TOPLINE

Serena leaned against the wooden counter that ran inside the window of her restaurant. It was one of those very rare moments when her business lay silent. A team member had gone to collect a missing item from the morning's delivery and the rest of the group hadn't arrived yet. The sun shone through the window and she closed her eyes, allowing its warmth to radiate across her face. The moment of tranquility didn't last long. The window shuddered as a hooded, bearded man knocked on the other side of the glass, close to where she had rested her head.

"Is this Becky's Breakfast?" he shouted through the glass as Serena jumped.

Another one. Serena rolled her eyes as she got up and walked to open the door to have a less noisy conversation with the destroyer of her peaceful moment. "Is this Becky's Breakfast?" the man asked again. "No—it's that spot over there," Serena responded, pointing towards the black door, the darkened windows, and the laminated sign on the door that said in indistinct writing—"FOOD DELIVERY DRIVERS: BECKY'S BREAKFAST."

The sign was put up every morning and taken down again just after lunch. Why? Because Becky's was only available in the mornings. The

rest of the time, the building opposite was host to one of the most laud-
ed fine dining restaurants in the city. A few hours from now, luxury cars
and an elegantly dressed assemblage of elite patrons would be lining up
for the best foie gras in town.

Serena headed back inside as the driver made his way across the street.
"A fine dining restaurant that sells breakfast sandwiches?" she pondered,
not for the first time. No matter—she had to get back to her office. The
real estate broker was due to visit in the next hour with new options for
her to expand into the east side of town. With a sigh, Serena wondered
whether it was worth her time. "He'll probably just show me the latest
list of properties for lease that I can't afford," she said to herself, wondering if she'd ever be able to grow beyond this one unit where her business
had thrived over these last three years.

Growing Your Restaurant

Independent restaurants have historically faced a tough road growing their
businesses. If one location is generating great consumer reviews, operating
well, and delivering profit, most restaurants will turn their sights on opening
a second. It's tough to do, and many restaurateurs bring on outside investors,
take a second mortgage on their home, or sign a personal guarantee on the
lease to make it work. But it seems worth it: twice the profit running the
same concept seems like a very good deal, if you can make it through the
start-up costs.

For the restaurant owners who are able to scrape together enough funds
to attempt it, the second location does pretty well, if not as well as the first,
and so they turn their sights on opening a third. This is where things begin
to break down. After spending millions of dollars on buildouts, lease guarantees, inventory load-in, and staff training to get the first three sites open,
the third does not do as well. The owners of the business find they cannot be
in three places at once, and perhaps operational execution or brand-standard
hospitality isn't consistent.

The solution to this problem? An above-restaurant operator. The problem
with this solution? The above-restaurant operator is underleveraged and

requires seven restaurants to manage. Millions of dollars later, the topline is struggling in the new restaurants.

The solution to this problem? An above-restaurant marketer. The problem with this solution? The marketer is under-leveraged, and requires at least 20 restaurants to market. And on it goes. For most restaurant concepts, the above-restaurant costs demand at least 100 locations to pay for them. And 100 locations, at a conservative $500,000 in start-up costs each, requires at least $50 million in capital to open.

The paths available to great restaurant brands have historically been to slowly bootstrap, to bring on outside investors, or to franchise, so that a different operator spends his or her capital on opening new restaurants. For this reason, many truly excellent restaurant brands have chosen to remain small, with one to two locations. In spite of guest requests to open another location in a nearby neighborhood, many restaurateurs look at the challenges of growth and choose to stick with the profitable establishment they have.

As a result, the big chains get bigger while the independents—except for a few breakout cases—remain individual locations. With their known brands, repeatable economic models, vast marketing budgets, and stable cash flow, the large chains don't face the same challenges of adding another unit. For the chains, their existence is itself a kind of moat. It is so hard to get to scale, that those already at scale have an advantage.

But as we detailed in Chapter 2 of *Delivering the Digital Restaurant*, our tastes are changing. Consumers are seeking more nutritious meals, eating in more dayparts, and embracing more international variety. Independent restaurants and small chains are innovating to meet this demand. Thus the challenges of growth and the demand for growth are going head to head. Ghost kitchens and virtual brands are two answers to this tension: how to grow without the headaches of opening new locations.

Ghost Kitchens vs. Virtual Brands

Both ghost kitchens and virtual brands give restaurants new tools to grow, but the terms are often conflated. Restaurants wondering if they are missing out on these growth trends may find it helpful to break the two ideas apart. Think of the ghost kitchen as the hardware, and the virtual brand as the software.

Ghost kitchens are the hardware that creates the underlying infrastructure for digitized restaurants. They are optimized for off-premise transactions. Unlike a standard restaurant, which is developed primarily to service dine-in customers, drive-thru customers, or perhaps a bit of takeout, the ghost kitchen excels at off-premise execution. Beyond that, it may be further customized for the needs of the brands it hosts—hood size, equipment type, storage needs, and so on. Still, it does not function without the software: in this case, the brands. The brands operating in the ghost kitchen could be either new, fully virtual brands or existing brick-and-mortar standbys.

Virtual brands are like the software that runs atop the computer hardware. Virtual brands can be run on ghost kitchen hardware, or on existing restaurants—often called "host kitchens." If the core host-kitchen restaurant menu is the primary piece of software, a virtual brand or two are like additional programs that allow the restaurant to use its hardware more fully. Several virtual brands can co-exist in a ghost kitchen or even in a traditional restaurant (or host) kitchen. The more brands (software) a ghost or host kitchen (hardware) is running, the more optimized that kitchen can be—busy during all dayparts, with different consumer segments, and on multiple occasions. Virtual brands and ghost kitchens can exist and thrive without each other being part of the same equation, or they can be combined into one.

When Does a Virtual Brand Make Sense?

Virtual brands are all about increasing revenue without creating complexity in the kitchen. By leveraging existing menu items, existing ingredients, and existing cooking processes, this model is all about operations doing what it already does, while marketing positions the resulting product differently for different consumer segments and dining occasions. The business model is therefore identical to the underlying restaurant.

Restaurants would do best to consider virtual brands once they have optimized their core offering, mastered their approach to digital marketing, and found efficiencies in operations for off-premise production. It is why virtual brands sit firmly at the back of our first book *Delivering the Digital Restaurant*.

Tip: What virtual brand cuisines complement your restaurant?

- You can't easily run Apple's Mail software on Microsoft's operating system. For the same reason, you have to figure out what food types complement your current operation.
- Find pairings of cuisine that represent different brand opportunities while utilizing common ingredients (e.g., sushi → poke).
- Determine underutilized cooking equipment and/or stations and find cuisines that could use up this capacity (e.g., fryer → wings, cold wells → salad).
- Consider different ways to market the same or similar product to entirely new audiences (e.g., a casual-dining pizza concept's salads rebranded to emphasize healthy lunch).
- If you want to try something completely different from your current cuisine, make sure you have the capacity to accommodate the additional complexity.

However, virtual brands have proliferated more significantly than we had initially anticipated at the start of the digital disruption. A combination of immature search algorithms, smart restaurateurs, and the pandemic created the perfect conditions for rapid adoption of virtual brands. As a result, virtual brands are now available to immediately play a substantial role in maximizing off-premise sales. There are several models to consider in taking advantage of this blossoming channel for restaurant revenue.

To determine whether virtual brands fit your restaurant, let's consider why they are an excellent option for restaurants to grow revenue.

1. **Serve small consumer niches:** Focus on niche cuisines that may not achieve the required volumes to make a full brick-and-mortar restaurant work.

2. **Increase capacity utilization:** Further penetrate the delivery trade radius with additional cuisines that drive

reach and frequency not possible with just the base brand.

3. **Search engine optimization:** Increase marketplace discoverability by taking up "digital shelf space" on the platforms and more narrowly targeting the virtual brand to things a consumer might search for.

4. **Capital-light brand expansion:** Grow geographically without the capex or operational overhead by sharing a strong brand with other restaurant operators.

We've developed a simple matrix that matches the different types of virtual brands to the profile of restaurants that fit each model best. First, select your restaurant's primary strength on the matrix's Y-axis (vertical line) below. Second,

Tip: Know your strengths. Assess your readiness.

- Before you rush to find your place on the matrix above, take a moment to reflect on your business's core strengths.

- Consider what causes you the most concern. Is it operational consistency? Cost management? Driving compelling marketing through fresh and engaging products or traffic-driving initiatives?

- Pick a growth path that leverages your strengths and minimizes your weaknesses. Expanding through the wrong vehicle will compound those weaknesses, not remove them.

- Signs you are strong in operations and execution include: clearly defined processes, clearly defined roles, consistent outcomes (product quality, speed, accuracy), and happy teams.

- Signs you are strong in brand and menu include: excellent online reviews, a strong recurring customer base, and a proactive marketing calendar.

- "It sounds easier to _________" is not leveraging your strengths. It is avoiding your weaknesses. Your growth path must leverage your strengths.

OPEX INVESTMENT / CAPITAL INTENSITY	LOW	MEDIUM	HIGH
BRAND & MENU	A. License to virtual restaurant licensor		D. Create virtual brands for others
BOTH			C. Create own virtual-brand for own restaurant
OPS & EXECUTION	B. License a virtual brand from licensor		

CORE EXPERTISE (row axis label)

Figure 5.1 Restaurant Growth Approaches: Virtual Branding Options

select the level of investment that your restaurant group is willing to make on the X-axis (horizontal line). The box corresponding to your restaurant's strengths and investment profile is the best approach for virtual branding for your restaurant. Below the matrix, we've described each model further.

A. LICENSE TO VIRTUAL RESTAURANT LICENSOR

If your own brand has great recognition beyond its geography, but expansion is beyond your own means, consider licensing it to a licensor, platform, or broker that matches the placement of your brand with the right operators. Franklin Junction and Meal Outpost do just this. Your own brand becomes virtual, but another company protects it by qualifying the right match between brand and operator. Similarly, these licensors manage ongoing compliance with the brand's expectations.

Franklin Junction's CEO, Rishi Nigam, believes, "Most restaurants function at 50 percent or less capacity." But he concedes, "I think sometimes restaurants don't realize they have extra capacity because they've been operating the same way for such a long time."[36] It is why, at Franklin Junction, their team offers a consultative approach to ensure the restaurant can genuinely handle a virtual brand and fit it appropriately to current activity. Nigam says,

> We have to balance not just a host kitchen's expectation, but a brand's expectation because they do have equity in the marketplace. And so you put a Nathan's Famous or Dickey's Barbecue somewhere, you can't just turn it on and off at a whim…A huge value we bring to brands, and not just host kitchens, is that the brand will be represented well.

Nigam notes his team undertakes mystery shopping and audits—much like a franchise team would for larger brands.

Meal Outpost takes a slightly different approach. They also partner with restaurant concepts that have proven themselves as high-performing off-premises brands. Instead of manually vetting host operators, Meal Outpost has built a seamless, transparent, and efficient way to connect and integrate with host restaurants online. Host restaurants can onboard themselves, search for a brand based on equipment, day part, ingredient overlap, and most importantly geography, and reserve the brand that fits their needs. Licensors can see who each host operator is and review verification data like kitchen photos and Google Business Profiles. If approved by the licensor, the host is onboarded and fulfills all off-premises sales channels established by Meal Outpost.

It is important to consider how much support is provided to ensure brand execution consistency, whether you're considering licensing your own brand or licensing from someone else. "We don't launch locations unless we put eyes on it and visit it ourselves. This is not a completely virtual program," Nigam adds. If you plan to license a brand, ensure you have the controls necessary to provide an appropriate fit and avoid brand equity dilution through less brand-compliant operators.

As the name suggests, the business model in this arrangement is a license deal. The licensing restaurant will receive a percentage of revenue. The broker will keep a portion of the revenue. And the restaurant operator will bear the capital, labor, and inventory risk but will also keep the profit upside.

Suits those seeking the Capital-Light Brand Expansion advantage

B. LICENSE A VIRTUAL BRAND FROM A LICENSOR

On the other side of the equation, you may be looking for alternative brands to complement your current offer or take advantage of spare capacity in your kitchen. The purveyors of virtual brands—including licensors like Franklin Junction, creators like Nextbite or Virtual Dining Concepts, or third-party marketplaces like Uber Eats and DoorDash—aim to provide incremental orders into a kitchen that is already operating.

The third-party platforms can utilize the extensive customer data from their platform to inform licensees which foods customers are searching for most frequently by zip code. UberEats and DoorDash can then pair the right brand with the right restaurant licensee in the right location. However, in this instance, the virtual brands are exclusive on just the third-party platform that created them. While on the positive side this means the platform can push the virtual brand in its algorithm; on the negative side, the virtual brand may not be available where all consumers shop—which is to say, other platforms.

Thinking about the reach of the virtual brand is an essential component. Selecting the right licensor is as much about the marketing support the licensor can provide as it is about the brand itself. Celebrity virtual brands have a particular advantage in this case, where the customer base is already both a fan of the celebrity and their endorsements. "At Virtual Dining Concepts, we pair the enticing combination of amazing food concepts with creators, influencers, celebrities, and media platforms that drive immediate levels of brand resonance to an already engaged community," says Stephanie Sollers of Virtual Dining Concepts.[37] "By tapping into this existing customer base, our restaurant and kitchen clients benefit from immediate revenue from a net-new audience." When the celebrities have significant influence on social, the promotional activity can be ongoing. "Our partners that have been with us for over a year continue to see sizable growth from our brands portfolio," Sollers continues.

Meal Outpost drives revenue through its catering program. Host operators fulfill catering orders initiated by Meal Outpost, which helps the performance of the license brand. Dustin Mares, Co-Founder of Meal Outpost says,

> All of our license partners are great catering brands, so we leverage that for host operators by proactively securing catering opportunities. It's a great way to drive top-line sales early on while third party marketplaces are just getting going. It's a great marketing channel if a brand is new to the trade area as well.[38]

Choosing the right brand is as much about the topline you believe it can drive, as it is about making sure that revenue does not come at too high a cost. While the various virtual branding companies say they put significant effort into matching the right brands to the right kitchens, ultimately you'll need to ensure the brand fits into your existing operation without creating unnecessary complexity. The core and virtual brands may share common ingredients, equipment, and staffing, reducing incremental costs.

In this business model, the restaurant operator bears any capital, labor, and inventory risk. The restaurant operator receives a portion of the revenue that is similar to the expected marginal profit after food costs, assuming that all other costs are fixed.

Suits those seeking to Serve Small Consumer Niches or Increase Capacity Utilization

 **Tip: Choose your licensor.**

- The same level of care should be taken in choosing a licensor as in choosing the brand.

- Make sure your agreement has "easy outs" should the licensor, brand, or host not hold up its promise.

- Clear articulation of standards, training, supply chain, and marketing support are important to understand before committing.

- Data on why the brand and cuisine type fits in your specific geographical location should be clear—ask for search queries or competing brand results.

C. CREATE OWN VIRTUAL BRAND FOR OWN RESTAURANT

When you have a firm grasp on digital marketing and operational deployment, and you're successfully executing for your core brand's off-premise sales, you may look at virtual brands as a means to benefit from your efforts in the virtual arena. Virtual branding in this way can range from quite basic—same items, new name—to much more complex.

The first, and easiest, method is to reposition your current menu items for a different customer base or occasion. An example of this method is a "salad" virtual brand that takes the salad from the core restaurant brand, changes the branding and product name, then markets it to an audience different from the core restaurant brand. For example, imagine a high-end premium steak brick-and-mortar dine-in restaurant brand positioned for traveling professionals in hip locations creating a dedicated salad brand targeting nearby office workers. Most office workers wouldn't think to order a salad from a steakhouse, and the steakhouse is likely underutilized in the morning, so this rebranding is a win-win. The salad brand marketed to office workers brings these customers a new option for lunch. And the salad prep occurs before the steakhouse gets busy.

For example, at Alfa Co, one of Saudi Arabia's most prominent restaurant groups, their casual dining Piatto brand has created a "virtual pizza" brand. Their virtual pizza brand enables the higher-end pizza offering through Piatto to continue to service its core customers while also servicing a delivery-optimized pizza concept with an alternative brand and value proposition. Additionally, it enables two spots of digital real estate on a marketplace, increasing the chance that a customer looking for pizza chooses one made from a Piatto kitchen.

The second, and slightly more complex, method is to develop an adjacent cuisine type that can utilize the ingredients already in your kitchen, but which is truly a different set of products. An example of an adjacent cuisine type could be a poke bowl virtual brand that takes many of the same ingredients from a sushi restaurant. The virtual brand then addresses the gaps for customers searching for poke online.

In our first book, we talked about UberEats rolling out poke concepts virtually in Chicago through sushi restaurants. Virtual restaurant expansion got the new trendy food from the coasts—where poke restaurants were popping up—to the middle—where poke restaurants hadn't yet been built.

The third, and most complex, method is to develop additional cuisine types that are dissimilar from the base brand and may require additional ingredients, but utilize similar cooking and preparation methods. An example of a new cuisine type might be a restaurant famous for its burgers that chooses to create a hot dog virtual brand. The toppings and menu preparation are all identical. All that the restaurant must add is hot dogs and hot dog buns.

In this model of virtual brands, all revenue goes to the restaurant as both the operator and the creator of virtual brands.

Suits those seeking the Search Engine Optimization and Capital Light Brand Expansion advantage

D. CREATE VIRTUAL BRANDS FOR OTHERS

Where your restaurant team's expertise lies in brand and menu development, you may even consider developing brands solely for the purpose of licensing out to other restaurant concepts. This is the business model of Nextbite and Virtual Dining Concepts. Restaurants, too, may see the opportunity of growing the restaurant brands or virtual offerings that they initially create for themselves into offers that could exist within other locations besides their own.

Wow Bao began this way. Created as a restaurant by Richard Melman and the Lettuce Entertain You team, Wow Bao first opened in 2003 with a compact 384-square-foot kiosk at the main entrance of Chicago's iconic Water Tower Place mall. Their brand is now one of the fastest growing concepts in the nation through licensing a smaller menu offering across the United States—opening over 500 "locations" in just 18 months through virtual branding.

In this business model, the brand creator receives the revenue and pays out a portion to the restaurant operator.

Suits those seeking the Capital-Light Brand Expansion advantage

When Does a Ghost Kitchen Make Sense?

Once your restaurant has established its brand, or collection of brands, the next question becomes: where to put it? Historically, the only way to grow unit count has been to work with a realtor to find a new location, spend hundreds of thousands (if not millions) of dollars converting the space to your brand standards, hire 30 to 50 employees, and then hope that the new location resonated with the surrounding population.

Ghost kitchens are certainly easier, cheaper, and faster to establish when compared to building and opening a new brick-and-mortar location. They require less labor than a brick-and-mortar location too. "The rapid growth we're seeing in ghost kitchens allows restaurants to expand more quickly and more cost-effectively than they ever could before. Ghost kitchens can open up a vast new opportunity that will only grow with time," says Atul Sood, Chief Business Officer of Kitchen United.[39]

But that is not to say that running a profitable ghost kitchen location is easier than running a profitable brick-and-mortar location. Remember, a ghost kitchen is a kitchen optimized for off-premise consumption, whose meals are accessed primarily—if not exclusively—in a digital format. To succeed in a ghost kitchen environment, an operator must be a savvy digital marketer with frictionless digital consumer engagement. A restaurant's digital marketing capability must be optimized to drive sufficient volume through digital channels. Assuming a restaurant has digital cracked, ghost kitchens are a very attractive, capital-light way to grow.

Many see ghost kitchens as a less capital-intense way to grow efficient food production capability. Some QSR giants, like Chick-fil-A, utilize ghost kitchens less than a mile from where they operate a brick-and-mortar location—solely because the brick-and-mortar location is full. They have reached peak throughput in their brick-and-mortar location—there are no more efficiencies to be gained—but building an additional full restaurant in such close proximity may not make sense. In this case, a ghost kitchen helps restaurants keep "open for orders" when they have already reached capacity. (Notably, Chick-fil-A is a practitioner of the Kaizen practices mentioned in Chapter 4, which is one reason why their restaurants are capable of producing over $10 million a year in sales.) Once a restaurant has optimized kitchen design, equipment selection, processes, and overall kitchen production workflow to an optimal level to satisfy multiple channel throughput (on- and off-premise), the operation can benefit from a nearby ghost kitchen. The next challenge is determining how.

In the first *Delivering the Digital Restaurant* Chapter 9 "Ghost Kitchens (Aren't that Scary)," we explored the different ghost kitchen models, and here, we'll take that a step further. Which ghost kitchen model is right depends on a restaurant's capabilities and goals. Some ghost kitchen models may be a fit with a particular restaurant, whereas others may not. Early on, the ghost kitchen dream was oversold to many excited potential restaurant owners; however, without the assistance needed to help these owners qualify themselves, many ghost kitchen operators failed.

There are five key reasons why a ghost kitchen may be a good idea for a restaurant brand:

1. **Expand capacity:** Create additional kitchen capacity near other full restaurants without the capital required for a full restaurant.

2. **Test products and concepts:** Obtain direct consumer feedback on new ideas without impacting the wider business.

3. **Increase reach and delivery speed:** Expand the restaurant's geographical spread in a capital-light manner.

4. **Prep ingredients in a commissary setting:** Complete bulk preparation in one place and distribute out to each unit.

5. **Improve consumer experience:** Fully optimize for off-premise delivery, reducing cost and improving the quality of consumer experience.

Ghost kitchens can serve more than one of the benefits represented above, but being clear on which is most important will help in the ghost kitchen model decision-making process.

We've developed a simple matrix that outlines the different types of ghost kitchens currently being offered and the profile of restaurants that fit each model best. First, select your restaurant's primary strength on the matrix's Y-axis (vertical line) below. Second, consider the level of investment that your restaurant group is willing to make and select this on the X-axis (horizontal line). The box corresponding to your restaurant's strengths and investment profile displays the best approach to virtual branding for your restaurant.

OPEX INVESTMENT / CAPITAL INTENSITY		LOW	MEDIUM	HIGH
CORE EXPERTISE	BRAND & MENU	A. License to ghost kitchen operator		
	BOTH	B. Hub & Spoke ghost kitchens	C. Full-service ghost kitchens	D. Fully integrated ghost kitchens
	OPS & EXECUTION		Operate a ghost kitchen yourself	Build own ghost kitchen facility

Figure 5.2 Restaurant Growth Approaches: Ghost Kitchen Models

A) License to Ghost Kitchen Operator

Where your brand is clearly defined, your menu established and successful, and your customers drawn to your offer, but where real estate development, multi-unit operational consistency, and execution remain a challenge, this ghost kitchen operation may be most suitable. This approach de-risks the complexity of getting started with ghost kitchens while removing the challenges of opening in markets where recruiting and training may be a barrier. An example of this type of arrangement is Wendy's deal with Reef. Reef's "vessels" (ghost kitchens) were developed and operated by Reef team members on behalf of the Wendy's brand.

As the name suggests, the business model in this arrangement is a license deal. The licensor brand will receive a percentage of revenue. The ghost kitchen operator will bear the capital, labor, and inventory risk but will also keep the profit upside.

Be wary, though—most restaurant brands that have established brand credibility want to protect that credibility, and ghost kitchen operators that seek to "manage multiple brands" from one ghost kitchen unit add potential risk unless prepping, cooking, and packaging are undertaken in separate areas. Here, your well-defined brand parameters, cooking processes, and quality expectations must be definitive, explicit, and detailed—much as they would be for a traditional franchise. This is because you're outsourcing the operational aspect of your brand to a third party—the ghost kitchen operator. Of course, trust and clear auditing are essential between the restaurant and the ghost kitchen operation.

Suits those seeking to Increase Reach & Delivery Speed

B) Hub & Spoke Ghost Kitchens

Where you consider your brand and operational capabilities as distinguishable strengths but where available resources to expand are limited, a hub & spoke ghost kitchen model might be worth exploring. At these locations, the food is "finished" in a quick, simple, and nimble manner before being sent out to customers that have ordered from within the delivery radius of the satellite location. This satisfies, therefore, both the "reach" and "speed" benefits but also requires trust and clear procedural and quality expectations as the ghost kitchen company handles the final steps of the cooking process before it is delivered to a guest. SAJJ Mediterranean has tried this approach with All Day Kitchens with a limited menu—enabling brand extension but through a smaller menu that can be executed within the confines of this approach.

The business model in this arrangement is the same as the model used for selling packaged food for pickup at the home restaurant location. The ghost kitchen purchases meals from the home kitchen "hub" for distribution across the "spokes" of its network. The ghost kitchen bears the inventory risk, which it manages through algorithmic forecasting.

Suits those seeking to Increase Reach & Delivery Speed

C) Full-Service Ghost Kitchens

Where there's a slightly higher budget available to invest in growth through ghost kitchens, and where operational control of a brand is considered critical, full-service ghost kitchens are worth considering. In these models, the ghost kitchen operator is like a landlord or a membership services provider. While these ghost kitchen operators do not cook the food, they provide services to help their restaurant partners—such as aggregator technology,

Tip: Driving revenue from a ghost kitchen.

- Without a brick-and-mortar presence, restaurants in ghost kitchens must drive sales exclusively through digital marketing.

- Succeeding in a ghost kitchen requires a strong brand, excellent marketplace SEO, time spent on A/B testing, and the willingness to spend money on digital marketing.

- Operating several brands out of a ghost kitchen may help a restaurant reach its desired sales.

- Some ghost kitchens invest in first-party ordering technology, others in kiosk-enabled take-out, and still others in third-party order aggregation to assist restaurant tenants in driving topline.

logistics optimization, digital marketing support, ware-washing, goods-in services, and front-of-house staff.

Although add-on services support restaurants as they adapt to the operational differences within a ghost kitchen, the critical factor is the location of the ghost kitchen itself. In Kitchen United's Series C funding round, much was made of some of their investors—Kroger, Circle K, Simon Property Group—one of the largest grocers, c-stores, and mall operators, respectively. These large companies have kitchen infrastructure, a regular flow of customers, and a desire to drive traffic beyond their core function. To capitalize on their well-located assets, they could add a Kitchen United ghost kitchen to their existing retail business. "We all know the adage: location, location, location—this remains true for all restaurants, whether in a traditional format or in a ghost kitchen. Hence, we're very particular when it comes to site selection," says Kitchen United's Sood.

In a full-service ghost kitchen, upfront capital costs are eliminated. While revenue and margins might be slightly lower due to third-party marketplace fees and the conversion of upfront capex to ongoing rent, the returns are infinite due to the zero upfront costs. The ghost kitchen operator takes the capex risk—signing a multi-year lease and financing the equipment and buildout. The tenants take the opex risk—the cost of labor is the most significant commitment (albeit minimal compared to a full brick-and-mortar). This labor investment, coupled with potentially lower margins, can make the breakeven revenue required to succeed higher than restaurants may expect. Some full-service ghost kitchen operators, like Kitchen United, provide additional sales channels to drive higher-margin sales—through their own app or walk-in ordering kiosks for guests to pick up the food themselves to offset this risk.

Full service ghost kitchens are also excellent for testing new products, cooking methods, and concepts, as long as the expectation for profit is minimal. For this purpose, these kitchens should be viewed as R&D, not as profit-generating units.

These kitchens can also be used as commissaries. While a commissary itself

Tip: Signs of a good ghost kitchen.

- Taste the food of several tenant restaurants after delivery. The whole model has been built for that channel, and if they are executing well, they should be delivering great food.

- Observe the site layout. Delivery requires great ingress (how drivers can get in) and egress (how they can get out). If drivers have to wait, how close, free, and plentiful is the parking?

- Observe the facility layout. What does it take to get finished food from the kitchen to the driver? Who is completing these steps (your restaurant staff, the facility staff, or automation)?

- Signage is also a factor to help drivers find the restaurants—does the ghost kitchen build their brand? Share which brands are included within it?

may not directly generate profit, it may enable surrounding units to be more profitable. Many scratch-cooking restaurants with multiple units have found that centralizing prep in a commissary can make the entire chain more profitable.

Suits those seeking any and all advantages of ghost kitchens

D. Fully Integrated Ghost Kitchens

Ghost kitchens rely on many components from the delivery ecosystem to be successful, such as great brand, great food execution, great location, great technology, great digital marketing, and great logistics. Fully integrated ghost kitchens aspire to achieve all these elements in-house, and do so by controlling each one. These types of ghost kitchens are still relatively rare because getting all these elements right can be complex and expensive. C3 has built and operates several delivery-enabled food courts full of its own brands, but has been slower to scale compared to other ghost kitchen models. ClusterTruck operates its own brands in its own facilities using its own technology but has focused on just a handful of core units. Crave has experimented with the idea of an integrated ghost kitchen, though it recently relocated from Idaho to Texas.

As hard as it sounds, getting it right can reap big rewards. These vertically integrated kitchens, purpose-built for digital off-premise consumption, may be able to bring quality, value, and convenience to consumers in a way that traditional brick-and-mortar restaurants and even other ghost kitchen models can't. For example, ClusterTruck is crushing what most restaurants are able to do through a third-party marketplace. Without charging consumers a delivery fee or menu markup, ClusterTruck delivers in an average time of 29 minutes for 26 percent of the cost of labor…including the cost of the delivery. It offers 15 different brands out of a single kitchen, enabling consumer repeat that all but the most favored brands are unable to achieve. Founder Chris Baggott says of the outcomes his ghost kitchen is able to achieve:[40]

> The secret is just what Amazon showed us: By having a purpose-built, fully integrated system that is aware of each resource required to produce and deliver a dish, ClusterTruck does not have under-utilization of equipment or staff. There is no latency

in the system. No one and nothing is ever waiting on any other dependency. The coordination happens entirely in the software.

A surprising number of restaurants during the pandemic became fully integrated ghost kitchens. Forced to shut their front-of-house and rely entirely on digital channels, these restaurants (usually entrepreneurial independents) added their own or licensed virtual brands to their kitchen. When the effects of the pandemic faded, but with labor still hard to come by, some of these restaurants shifted permanently to become fully integrated, multi-concept ghost kitchens. These innovators foreshadow what's to come for the industry.

Suits those seeking to Improve Consumer Experience

The most profitable growth is often the easiest. Throughout this section we have counseled you to do more of what you excel at, while minimizing your weakest points. If growing requires becoming good at something you've historically shied away from, consider if doing so is realistic, and what it would take. Some restaurants may find that neither virtual brands nor ghost kitchens are right for them. Rather, extending their same brand, from their same location, to their same customers into new occasions (e.g., catering) and new dayparts (e.g., breakfast) may be far easier.

SUMMARY: GROW TOPLINE

- Virtual brands are like software. Ghost kitchens are like hardware.

- Virtual brands can help drive revenue but shouldn't add material complexity or the additional revenue will not be profitable.

- Virtual brands can serve small niches, utilize capacity more effectively, take up digital shelf space and support capital-light expansion.

- There are four different virtual brand approaches: license to a licensor, license from a licensor, create your own for yourself, or create your own for others.

- Ghost kitchens are easier, cheaper, and faster to build than new brick-and-mortar locations and require less labor to run once open.

- Running a profitable ghost kitchen location requires digital marketing competence.

- Ghost kitchens can help restaurants expand capacity, test items and concepts, increase reach and delivery speed, prep in bulk, and improve the consumer experience.

- There are four different ghost kitchen approaches: license to a ghost kitchen operator, hub & spoke, full-service, or fully integrated.

  **TIME FOR REFLECTION!**

CHAPTER 5: GROW TOPLINE

1. What "similar" cuisine types to your current offer could be supported through your current kitchen and operational processes (e.g. poke to sushi, hot dogs to burgers, Mediterranean to salads)?

2. What small consumer niche food types (e.g., vegan pancakes, southern Indian curries) would fit your local customer demographic?

3. How many additional orders of an entree that takes less than 10 minutes to produce (from your existing menu) could your kitchen handle in an hour without needing incremental labor or equipment, and without each item going above the 10-minute prep time? Estimate or test the answer (A) at your quietest time of the week and (B) at the busiest time of the week.

4. Calculate the revenue potential of (A) and (B) from above. The sum (C) gives you an indication of the theoretical revenue potential of a brand that could sit on top of your current cuisine without adding complexity, cost or throughput inefficiency. Would the effort of producing another product (from a virtual brand) be a more effective means to reach that revenue potential versus what it would take to drive the same amount from your current brand?

5. If the incrementality of a virtual brand is appealing to you based on the answers to the previous questions, which type of growth strategy works best for you and why?

    A: License to virtual restaurant licensor

    B: License a virtual brand from a licensor

    C: Create own virtual brands for own restaurant

    D: Create own virtual brands for others

6. Rank the following five benefits of a ghost kitchen in order of what is most important to you now to what is least important (the highest being the most important). Why did you place the first item first? Why is the last item last?

    A: Expand capacity in a capital-light manner

    B: Testing products/concepts

    C: Increase reach/delivery speeds

    D: Improve bulk preparation/commissary efficiencies

    E: Improving off-premise consumer experience

7. If the efficiency of growing through ghost kitchens is appealing to you, which of the following suits your ghost kitchen expansion strategy best?

A: Have someone else operate the concept in a ghost kitchen

B: Have ingredient preparatory work completed in one location and distributed from there

C: Utilize other ghost kitchen infrastructure so that you can focus your team on cooking

D: Develop a ghost kitchen yourself so everything can be designed around one optimal system

8. What would be important to do more of, less of, or differently compared to how you do digital marketing today so that you can succeed with virtual brands or ghost kitchens?

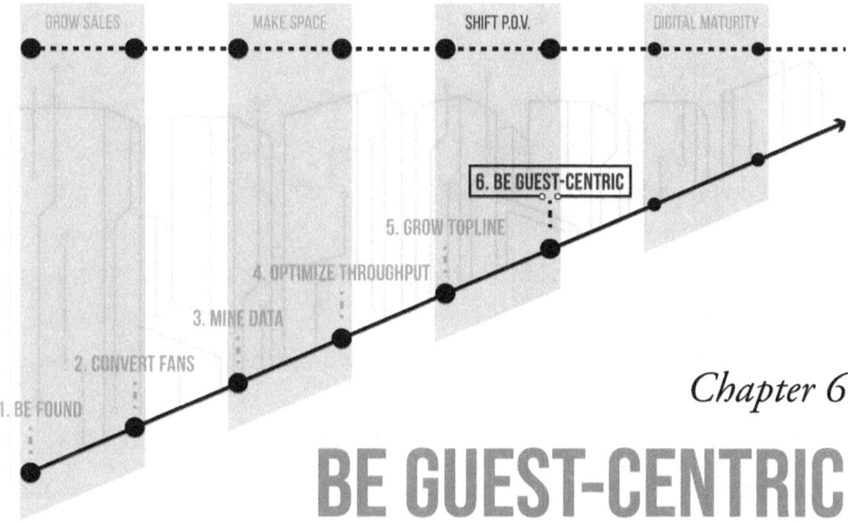

Chapter 6

BE GUEST-CENTRIC

Seventeen-year-old Luis was finally practicing to get his drivers' license. His parents were not surprised at his previous lack of interest—Luis used his bicycle, the bus, food delivery, and ride-sharing as his primary modes of transport. To him a car seemed expensive, inconvenient, and perhaps a little unsafe. Now his latest interest—playing guitar in a band—demanded that he be able to travel farther than usual, later than usual, while carrying something heavier than usual (his guitar). He conceded a car was perhaps the best solution and started driving lessons.

One day, while driving with his grandmother in the passenger seat, she suggested they go to Starbucks. That had been a favorite outing of theirs when Luis was younger, and she thought the experience of navigating the tight turns in the busy parking lot to get through the drive-thru would be good practice for him.

When they got to the order box, Luis looked at his grandmother. "I'll have a vanilla latte," she said.

He backed up in his seat so she had a direct view of the box, and whispered to her, "I'll have a dragon fruit refresher."

"Why are you telling me?" she asked.

"I'm not talking to her," he replied, gesturing at the disembodied voice coming through the box.

Luis's grandmother smiled. She remembered that, 50 years ago, when the drive-thru was new, talking to the box seemed a bit novel, if not odd. "Apparently," she thought, "to today's teenager, talking to a person seems a bit novel, if not odd."

"It's just like ordering in the store. It's the driver's responsibility to order," she told Luis.

"But I don't order in the store. I've never ordered in the store. I always order on the app."

Cars were piling up behind them. Luis's grandmother leaned over him and said loudly, "One vanilla latte and one dragon fruit refresher, please."

"But Grandma, I won't get my stars!" Luis exclaimed.

The definition of a digital restaurant is being where your consumers are. And increasingly, consumers are on their devices. The average American consumer spends six hours each day on their phones, tablets, and computer,[41] and they have become accustomed to interfacing with the world through their mobile devices. So much so that, for many common tasks, they strongly prefer a computer interface to a traditional face-to-face interaction. Restaurants have arrived late to this transition, which happened first in banking, then in travel, and next in retail. Just as the idea of standing in a line to talk to a person to cash a check has become anachronistic. So, too, will be the idea of talking to a human to order a latte.

To some, this future sounds cold. Where is the human connection of talking with someone about the weather or their day? Where is the predictability of seeing the same barista each morning? Where is the delight of the barista's smile when he gets your joke? Punching a button on a phone just does not come with the experience that we all imagine when we think of a coffee house. But to others, notably the younger others like Luis, why would anyone expect a human connection out of ordering coffee? Wouldn't it be better, and faster, to get a 100 percent consistent order by pushing a few buttons and leave the human connection to the person you brought with you to get a treat, or the person you are video chatting with while you drink your coffee?

While the primary focus in the first *Delivering the Digital Restaurant* and this companion playbook is the rise of the off-premise channel for restaurants, it would be remiss not to emphasize the extensive rise of digitization for the on-premise guest experience too. Why? Because consumers don't specialize in a single channel. Consumers use different modes of purchase for different occasions. A consumer may discover you online, but they may choose to experience you on future occasions through other channels. They may discover one brand and then, because of your packaging marketing, discover one of your virtual brands.

Regardless of the occasion, consumers expect what digital offers. They expect the ordering process to be similar from channel to channel. They expect the same, frictionless ease whether they choose to dine in, pick up, or have an item delivered. They increasingly expect experiences personalized to them as they cross channels.

Retail is farther ahead on the journey to omnichannel. While the landscape is by no means settled, retailers have declared their fulfillment strategies. Some, like Amazon and digitally-native brand Dollar Shave Club, have done it by specializing in digital relationships with consumers and eliminating the need for a brick-and-mortar experience. Or they have gone in the opposite direction—like local boutiques—to create an experience that can only be had in person. Others, like Walmart, have realized that the only way to optimize each channel is to create different physical and logistical pathways for each, while capturing the consumer data necessary to create a common consumer experience through their membership program Walmart+, or through telephone numbers and credit cards.[42] A few, like Nordstrom and Target,[43] have completely blurred the lines between channels, resulting in an in-store experience and an online experience that is each less efficient, effective, and pleasurable than it could be.

Restaurants have gone through a very rapid evolution. Just ten years ago, a restaurant had at most two channels: drive-thru and counter service in QSR; phone calls and internet orders for pizza; or dine-in and take-out in casual dining. In the last five years, accelerated by the pandemic, restaurants have felt the need to be everything to everyone. To date, most restaurants have chosen to see delivery as incremental to the base dine-in business, and therefore omnichannel purchasing has been tied to omnichannel fulfillment. Restaurants are just starting to see what retail already discovered: that specialization is even an option.

The situation is easiest for upscale, experience-driven, dine-in restaurants. These restaurants can opt out of delivery, digital interfaces, and the world of convenience. They can rely on servers to create a personalized experience, supported by loyalty programs that track guests' preferences, reservation platforms that sell the best seats at the best times, and hand-held POS terminals so that servers spend less time walking back and forth to the kitchen and more time talking with guests.

Chain delivery pizza restaurants, at the opposite end of the spectrum, also have things fairly easy. With nearly 100 percent of their sales coming through digital platforms and all of their product consumed off-site, the only blurred lines these outlets need to handle is the occasional consumer who prefers to pick up themselves rather than receive delivery.

In the middle, from QSR to fast-casual to casual dining, are restaurants that offer ordering online, in-store, at the drive-thru, over the phone, through first-party and third-, at the table, on a kiosk, on a tablet, or with a human. These restaurants, whether chain or independent, have so many interfaces with their guests that confusion reigns. On the fulfillment side, the situation can be even worse. The experience expectations of each order channel are different. The time expectations of each channel are different. The mode of fulfillment of each channel is different.

There are three issues here. First, how can a restaurateur ensure guest data is captured accurately regardless of channel? Second, how can they make each ordering process—whether online, in-store, or through the drive-thru, whether tech-enabled or with a human—feel similar? And third, how can they optimize the physical four walls to deal with so many different types of behavior?

Capturing Guest Data

The same consumer may use a third-party system to order for an office lunch on Monday, use click 'n' collect on her way home from work on

Thursday, and choose to dine-in with a friend on Saturday. She may be using the same restaurant brand in different ways to satisfy different needs, but she is still the same person.

However, from the restaurant's point of view, it may appear that a consumer has lapsed from the brand simply because today, they've chosen to order third-party, whereas on other days, they order first-party for pickup.

"It has never been more important for any operator to think about 'How do I have a single view of the consumer' whether they walk in, pick up the phone, or use my digital channels," says Ilir Sela, founder and CEO of Slice, a first-party ordering digital enabler for independent pizza places. "What happens today is that, when a consumer decides to switch their channel, their journey starts over with your shop." That's not good for the restaurant or for the consumer. Sela continues, "It's incredibly important for every operator to have a view of their customers and make sure the consumer has a consistent experience regardless of channel."[44]

A Customer Data Platform (CDP) is a tool for marrying data from different channels to create a 360-degree, customer-centric view. According to Bounteous, a digital experience agency, a CDP is more than a "newly-spun acronym for what was once called a CRM (Customer Relationship

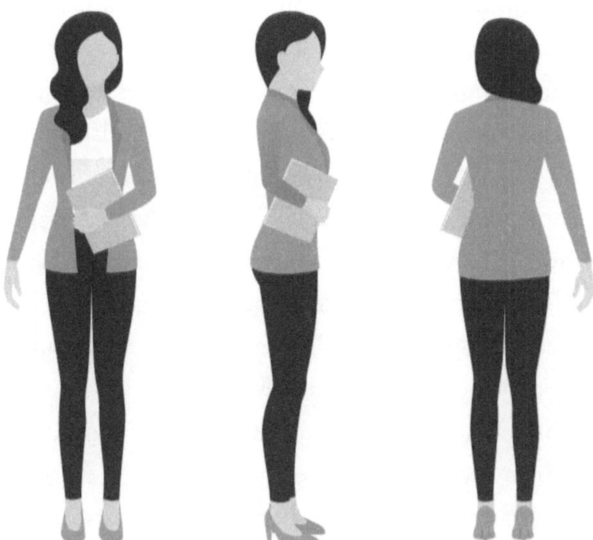

Figure 6.1 The Omnichannel Guest — One Person, Three Views

Tip: Personalize each channel.

- Consider the consumer journey in your primary channel (the one comprising most of your sales). What makes it great? How is that channel personalized to each guest?

- Consider your secondary channels. Are they as good as the primary? As personalized?

- What information is used to enable the personalization (e.g., do your team members just inherently know the regulars, or is there a record in your reservation system like OpenTable that can record customer purchasing preferences on previous visits?). Are those information sources recorded? Connected across channels?

Management)." They go on to say, "A CDP enables a retailer to create detailed profiles of their customers, and analyzes their journeys and buying behavior while handling multiple data points from a variety of sources. With this wealth of data available, a unified customer database can combine the data from these various channels to build a more complete profile of each customer. These profiles can then be leveraged by other systems."[45]

Abhinav Kapur, Founder and CEO of Bikky, a restaurant-specific CDP, says, "Restaurants have always been a relationship-driven business. The foundation of a restaurant is the experience guests have when they walk in the door, and now with delivery that they have at home." Kapur continues, "With the growth of delivery, the growth of e-commerce, the growth of pay-at-table, a brand can now collect all the data these channels are throwing off and centralize it in one place so they can paint a true picture of who their guests are, what they are doing, when they are ordering, how frequently they are ordering, how valuable they are, all the way down to nitty-gritty things like what are their menu item preferences, did they eat something that caused them to not come back, did they convert on a specific promotion, did that promotion influence their behavior over the long-term."[46]

Tip: Clean data in = clean data out.

- In Chapter 3, we offered the same tip for product-level data. Now apply the same lesson to customer data.
- Ensuring your customer data is clean before combining it together with sources from other channels will get you more out of a CDP.
- Some CDP providers will support the efforts to clean customer data as part of their onboarding process.

A CDP enables a restaurant to bring all guest data together into one place to truly understand, engage, and retain guests. As Kapur explains, "Most restaurants are probably only in the position to leverage this data as it relates to online ordering or pay-at-table because those are digital transactions. While that is the fastest growing part of the business, the fact is that the largest part of the business is in-store."

Newer cloud-based POS systems understand the value of this data and make it available to CDP providers—but unless a consumer has opted into a loyalty program, the type of data available on each transaction is likely to be limited. Part of what a CDP does is clean the data. As an example, Kapur says that at Bikky, "We try to de-dupe every single customer record. How many customers are you serving? What's your repeat rate? How does that vary across locations? We need a clean record to paint a true picture of your guest. Without doing the data scrubbing, you are adding a lot of noise to the system. Restaurants are in a position now where they can't afford to not know the answer to these questions."

"Customers who order through multiple channels are three times more valuable than a regular customer," says Kapur. But a restaurant wouldn't know who these guests are without a CDP to combine the records of customers from a variety of different channels.

> Loyalty is the absolute bottom of your funnel," says Kapur. "10 to 20 percent of a restaurant's guests are likely to sign up for a loyalty program. There is always a ceiling to how many guests you can engage. We give you insight on this other 80 percent. If you just look at the loyalty program, you are going to get such a skewed perspective—either super-engaged or looking for discounts. By sitting in between the POS and the loyalty program, we can help put the two together.

A CDP is certainly powerful, but it is also expensive. It can be a difficult investment to justify for smaller restaurant groups and independents. In addition, your restaurant team will need to have someone that can harness the capabilities of a CDP system. A chain can spread that resource across multiple units, but an independent restaurant may have to settle for utilizing other SaaS systems that incorporate autonomous marketing outreach functionality.

Once the CDP is in place or you have functionality that comes close, the data is clean, and guests are known across channels and you can pinpoint each guest down to the individual transaction, intelligent remarketing can truly begin. Did that guest really abandon the brand? Or did they simply have a baby and start ordering delivery instead of coming to the restaurant? Knowing the answer to that question impacts the marketing message that the customer receives. Instead of showering the guest with win-back discounts in a series of "spray and pray" unread emails or text messages, Kapur says, "You can thank them for making the effort to stay with your brand even as their lives changed and the occasions in which they used your brand changed."

The goal of clean data, stored in a CDP or otherwise, is to segment your existing guests and re-market to them in a way that is relevant, timely and consistent. DoorDash has released an excellent white paper called "The Ultimate Guide to Restaurant Email Marketing."[47] They, and other marketplaces and first-party ordering tools, have put tremendous energy into creating free resources for restaurants to up their game on many fronts—and digital marketing is one of them.

The value of having a first-party ordering platform is not just for off-premise ordering. It's about capturing the guest's order no matter how they choose

Tip: Re-marketing work flows can be powerful.

- A CDP can help segment your customers based on behavior. Past behavior is the most significant predictor of future behavior. Segments could include new customers, frequent customers, lapsed customers, customers by channel, or customers by promotional response.

- Developing workflows to market different incentives to different behavioral segments enables you to deliver relevant messages at the right time to maintain or grow your relationship with them.

- Understanding a customer's behavioral data—what they buy, where they buy, how they buy, etc.—means your offers can be targeted to the behavior each customer prefers.

- You can automate offers based on rules and workflows that are complex to undertake manually, but seamless to undertake through autonomous software.

- An email marketing tool, such as Mailchimp, Active Campaign, or Constant Contact, may be sufficient to get you started.

- The A/B testing concept from Chapter 3 can also be applied to remarketing emails and text messages.

to dine with you. The digital restaurant ultimately enables you to serve guests wherever they choose. Therefore, a digital interface for on-premise ordering must be part of the future. While the on-premise guest still enjoys the "human" presence and being served, the customer data acquired through other channels or previous purchases can help inform the server of guest preferences. Understanding your guest's dietary preferences, allergies, previous purchases, seating preferences, likelihood to order complementary items, bias toward core menu items or limited-time offers, and frequency of visit will all be data points that can act as briefing notes to enable a server to create the very best on-premise experience. This can start with table reservation software all the way to loyalty QR identifiers to "check in" at a table.

Enabling a guest to know you value their loyalty and remember them is the equivalent of what the very best servers do today through memory alone. When a menu for on-premise computes these factors on a human's behalf, the customer is getting an enhanced experience—much like they enjoy when they utilize the third-party marketplace home screens. No wonder 56 percent of Gen Z customers prefer engaging through a QR code.

Of course, to measure all of these consumer behaviors across channels, all channels must be digital. Restaurant online ordering company Olo describes the future as "the digital entirety," meaning that all restaurant transactions must eventually be digitized in some way. Olo's CEO, Noah Glass, told us, "As it stands, only about 15 percent of today's restaurant orders are digital. Even more, the majority of transactions are nameless and impersonal, despite how many times a guest frequents a location. As we look to the future, we believe technology has the opportunity to touch and add value to 100 percent of restaurant orders—on- and off-premise—to best serve guests, operators, and stakeholders within the trillion-dollar industry. This transition to digital entirety will equip brands with the direct insight to gain a deeper, 360-degree understanding of their guests, including their likes, dislikes, and habits; inform smart business decisions; build meaningful connections; and deliver more personalized hospitality that makes every guest feel like a regular."[48] This digitization creates the data that sophisticated restaurant brands need to view their consumer holistically.

Glass's comments show how restaurants and the technology companies that support them are both moving towards greater maturity at a pace determined by the rate of adoption from one and the speed of innovation from the other. As guest data is utilized to enhance the consumer experience, greater understanding of the financial value of guest data utilization becomes possible. Glass's vision for digital entirety seems a very real end-state; however, how fast it emerges will depend on how quickly restaurants adopt digital ordering for on-premise occasions.

Harmonizing Consumer Journeys across Channels

The second part of omnichannel behavior—a consumer's expectations of a brand from one channel carrying over into others—means on-premise transactions must be as frictionless as their off-premise counterparts. For quick-serve and casual dining restaurants, this likely means an ordering and pay process (kiosk, pay-at-table) that is very similar, if not identical to, the off-premise process (mobile, app).

Embedding digital consumer self-service into the physical restaurant via pay-at-table mobile or tablet, kiosk ordering, or QR codes ensures that every guest is a known guest, every time. It also makes cross-channel loyalty completely seamless for the consumer. Companies GoTab and Presto both offer a tablet that integrates with the POS and kitchen to enable consumers to place orders and close out the bill themselves or with a live server, depending on their preferences. The order information transfers across all devices so that a guest need not wait to order another drink or pay the bill, but they can order their entrée through a server who can share details about the dishes. And, regardless of the payment method she chooses, the guest knows exactly what to do because the consumer journey is similar in each channel.

Through the pandemic, QR code-enabled menus were a necessity where restaurants needed to provide no-touch solutions. Unfortunately, their rush to deployment created a surge of PDF menus, leading to a poor customer experience. The customer had to do something they weren't accustomed to—use their phone to access the menu. Then they experienced further difficulties, connecting to Wi-Fi where their signal was weak and reading a menu on a device smaller than their hand.

No surprise, then, that restaurants quickly scaled back the use of QR code-enabled menus as the pandemic subsided. According to PYMENTS' findings from the 2022 edition of PYMNTS Restaurant Readiness Index,[49] created in collaboration with Paytronix, the share of eateries offering the ability to place orders at the table using a QR code fell 17 points from 42 percent in September 2021 to 25 percent in April 2022. It's quite possible that had the restaurants had in place the foundational elements covered earlier, QR ordering could have linked into loyalty, pay-at-table, and personalized digital menus. Had that been the case, more consumers, and therefore more restaurants, would have been interested in keeping QRs around.

In contrast, mobile payment through a mobile wallet or a service such as PayPal or Venmo is increasingly becoming a standard means to pay for

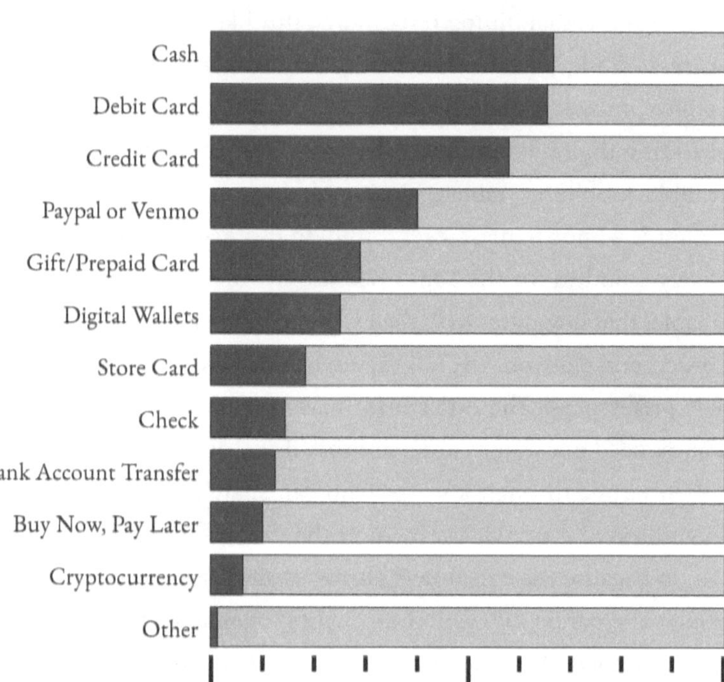

Source: PYMNTS.com | Credit Card Surcharges: Customer Experience and Choice, June 2022 | N = 5,197: Whole sample, fielded March 8, 2022 - March 29, 2022

Figure 6.2 How United States Consumers Pay at Retail Stores or Restaurants

everyday purchases. Why? It's easy. Double-clicking a phone to process a payment through fingerprint or facial ID verification is more straightforward than having to wait for the check, take out your wallet, compute the tip, sign the bill, and wait while the card or change is returned. It's also easier to use these same interfaces to split the check and share the cost between a group by items purchased. The restaurant benefits from digital payment functionality, too. It can shorten the table turn time and reduce the burden of cash handling and potential errors while further supplementing specific information on the customer's spending profile.

As ordering and payments become more digital in the physical space, consumers will flow seamlessly from one experience to another. They will be able to use the channel most appropriate for the occasion without having

Tip: Pay-at-table can improve the experience.

- Pay-at-table through guest tablet or server handheld can provide guests with the service they want without delay—including paying the bill.

- Tying a pay-at-table interface to the same interface used for off-premise occasions increases customer adoption and ties customer data affiliation across channels.

- Pay-at-table should incentivize the customer to provide an identifier (email/ cell number).

- Formulating a holistic view of an omnichannel guest for outreach/ LTV determination is worthy of a decent incentive if needed (e.g., free appetizer when they pay at table).

to learn a new interface. This has been difficult in the restaurant industry to date because of the stage of innovation it has been in. More often than not, different technology providers have been responsible for the kiosk vs. the app vs. POS vs. the pay-at-table tablet.

Accommodating Omnichannel within the Four Walls

As we've seen, for reasons of data collection and consumer ease of use, the ordering and payment methods must be similar across channels. But fulfillment methods do not have to be the same from channel to channel.

The first question a restaurant must resolve on omnichannel fulfillment is: does food ordered online come out of the same kitchen as food ordered onsite? Thus far, most restaurants have said: yes, it does. While there are a few ghost kitchens out there today focused exclusively on online orders, the model has not yet taken off. The primary reason is just as Service Physics indicated: most restaurant kitchens have excess capacity, leaving most restaurants motivated to use that capacity to serve multiple channels rather than trying to build new capacity dedicated to different channels.

This issue has led to a second question: how does a restaurant separate out the flow of orders to ensure the best experience for each channel, even when all orders are being fulfilled in the same place?

Recalling the history of drive-thrus as laid out in Chapter 3 of the first *Delivering the Digital Restaurant*, QSRs ultimately solved the different needs of drive-thru and dine-in customers by creating different production lines within the same kitchen, then optimizing the function of each line for the demands of the channel it served. For example, the production line serving the drive-thru keeps the menu item assembly separate so that it can be timed to the order flow coming through the order box. Items are complete just as the car that placed the order makes it through the "stack" between the order box and the pickup window.

Since the pandemic, large QSRs have started innovating the drive-thru order journey. Taco Bell introduced the Defy restaurant design, with production on the second floor and multiple pick-up lanes organized by channel below (order onsite vs. mobile order ahead and pickup). Shake Shack, historically a fast-casual with no drive-thru, created a drive-thru prototype with multiple lanes, again organized by channel. Chipotle went even further, creating the "Chipot-lane," which only allows for mobile order-ahead pickup. As of 2022, 80 percent of its new restaurant openings included a Chipot-lane.[50]

Independent restaurants are more likely to be a dine-in or fast-casual format without a drive-thru. But the lessons gained through the innovation in drive-thru apply equally to dine-in. If a restaurant chooses to use the same kitchen to produce orders for different channels, how does it fulfill these orders to protect the experience of each channel?

Examples of poor execution abound. For many restaurants, forced into embracing takeout and delivery as a matter of survival during the pandemic, the dining room became an impromptu off-premise expo station. Restaurants turned up dining room lights to help expo workers ensure order accuracy. Takeout packaging piled up on tables, chairs, and host desks. Drivers and take-out guests created a continual stream of people entering and exiting the dining area.

While this may have been okay during the pandemic as an emergency measure, it is decidedly not okay now that guests want to return to dining in. Takeout and delivery orders have not abated as dining rooms have filled up again, and clearly these two streams need separation to adequately serve each.

Restaurants can improve the experience of each channel without implementing any technology. Making room in the back-of-house for off-premise expo and including purposeful pickup shelving are two quick and easy changes that many restaurants have already made. For those restaurants with space-constrained kitchens, using screens or walls to hide front-of-house expo stations can be a solution.

After these easy wins, technology further enhances the experiences of each fulfillment channel. Technologies like geofencing—a location-based service that uses GPS, near-field communication, cellular data, or Wi-Fi to trigger an action when a customer, driver, or team member arrives or leaves a geographic area—can help time the orders, reducing the amount of finished but not-picked-up product to deal with. Technologies like text-message dynamic coded lockers can help separate the orders, ensuring the right order goes to the right customer. And technologies like order boards can help guests and drivers alike know the status of the order they are picking up.

Knowing when you're about to be busy before you're busy may sound far fetched, but being able to anticipate sales can ready your kitchen and improve speed of service. Geofencing technology isn't exactly new. The marketplaces use it to determine which drivers should be paired with which restaurant orders while enhancing trip efficiencies. Large restaurant chains have been utilizing it for many years, too. For example, in an attempt to drive app downloads, Burger King offered one-cent Whoppers "to customers who downloaded the brand's app and came within 600 feet of a McDonald's." "Location services have always played a critical role in creating best-in-class customer experiences," says Coby Berman, co-founder and Chief Operating Officer at Radar, bringing this experience to brands like Whataburger, Panera Bread, and Peet's Coffee.

These brands are now actively using geofencing solutions to help drive improved efficiency for their team to provide live ETAs, arrival detection, and prompt order firing for pickup and drive-thru occasions. This leads to more freshly made orders, with better temperatures and ultimately more

Tip: Geofence to tie driver arrival to fire-time.

- If your food deliveries are waiting for a delivery driver to show up, you're probably cooking as orders come in, rather than when orders should go out.
- With an understanding of the driver location through geofencing and arrival time, orders can be timed to the arrival of the driver.
- Less driver waiting time will encourage more drivers to be in your restaurant's red zone, thereby improving the fulfillment rate resulting in higher order volumes.

satisfied consumers. Guests that download a restaurant's app with enabled functionality can then use this same technology to unlock offers pushed to them via app or SMS text messages when they are in close proximity to a restaurant. They also remove friction from an app's ordering process by knowing where the nearest store is without burdening the prospective guest to locate it themselves. Panera Bread has also enabled its app to automatically identify guests' specific loyalty membership. Note—all of these benefits aid in driving the guest to utilize the first-party ordering platform, thereby driving higher margin and potentially incremental orders.

Forward-thinking restaurants are then looking to solutions from e-commerce, like Shipday or Cartwheel, to choose the best delivery logistics provider from among the options available. This automatic selection is set to maximize restaurant and guest experience rather than the efficiency of one marketplace platform.

More trips per hour for drivers improves the wider system efficiency for marketplaces. This supports overall driver happiness because, without it, driver churn can occur, adding more cost and complexity to the system. With drivers feeling more satisfied through more trips per hour, larger batched "baskets" from multiple vendor pickups, and non-peak time non-food deliveries, marketplaces are taking steps to improve their profitability. But a human driver can undertake only so many trips per hour. For this reason, research and innovation continues to explore non-human delivery solutions such as drones or autonomous sidewalk vehicles. If these technologies can lower the cost of the delivery, then restaurants, marketplaces, and consumers will all be better off.

Regardless of the technologies chosen to improve the guest experience, clarity for each channel is key. Guests need to know where to go and what is expected of them. The more unclear guests are, the more they will ask questions of otherwise-engaged employees, get frustrated, and potentially not return. For example, in an effort to fit pickup shelves into their front-of-house without significant capex, several restaurant chains have chosen to face the shelves perpendicular to the front door. While this is not a problem in itself, if one then hangs the sign above the shelves, it will not be visible from the front door. Delivery drivers and pick-up guests are left wondering, "Where is the food?"

As the industry goes further through the digitization journey, much as with the increased sophistication of the drive-thru early on, restaurant design will evolve to separate out the different fulfillment paths. Some restaurants will decide to not change a thing, only optimizing for on-premise customers. Others will reorient the kitchen to accommodate multiple lines and clear and efficient consumer handoff points. However, a new type of restaurant is also emerging—one that promises to provide more value than any format that came before it, and which will require rethinking the current model of restaurant operation—and that's what we'll cover next.

SUMMARY: BE GUEST-CENTRIC

- A digital restaurant is being where your consumers are. And they are on their phones.

- Consumers expect consistent frictionless experiences regardless of which channel they choose to interact with your brand through.

- The more channels your restaurant participates in, the higher the chance of additional complexity.

- A customer data platform allows you to track customer behavior across channels and then segment customers to communicate with them through autonomous workflows.

- Pay-at-table and other digital in-store ordering helps acquire data from the dine-in channel and provide a consistent ordering experience regardless of channel.

- Consider improvements to how different channels are fulfilled whether those improvements stem from the kitchen make-line or the pick-up points in the front of house.

  **TIME FOR REFLECTION!**

Chapter 6: BE GUEST-CENTRIC

1. Think practically about small steps you can take toward giving your guest a better experience, and what data you need to make it happen. Personalization demonstrates hospitality. How can your restaurant make your guests feel like you've "seen" them? For example, how should late deliveries be treated compared to normal orders? How should first-time app customers be treated compared to loyal regular users? What could you do to improve personalization to your guest orders tomorrow, next week, next month, or in the next year?

TOMORROW:

NEXT WEEK:

NEXT MONTH:

NEXT YEAR:

2. What is your business case for a CDP, keeping in mind that it will cost $10k to $50k a year plus a resource to fully utilize it? If the business case doesn't stack up for your restaurant, what steps can you take to consolidate your customer data into one place and use it as and when you are able?

3. Once a decision for a CDP is made, rank the list below—starting with the greatest area of opportunity to address through your new functionality and ending with the least-critical area. Why did you choose this order of ranking?

New customer retention

Improved visit frequency

Higher check average

Higher customer LTV

Lapsed customer recovery

4. If you utilize pay-at-table (order and pay) technology today, speak to three guests who have used it. Ask them what they like about using it and ask them what could be better. If you don't offer it, find and visit a nearby restaurant that does. Ask one of their servers what they like about it and what could be better. Consider using digital in-store ordering if you don't today. If you do, modify your process and configuration based on what you learned.

5. During a busy delivery window, calculate the average wait time for delivery drivers. Is the wait over 5 minutes ? If so, why? What could be done to ensure drivers don't have to wait at all while also ensuring the food isn't waiting for them to pick up?

6. What elements of your pick-up area could be improved to add a better experience for your dine-in guests and for your take-out customers/drivers collecting on behalf of customers?

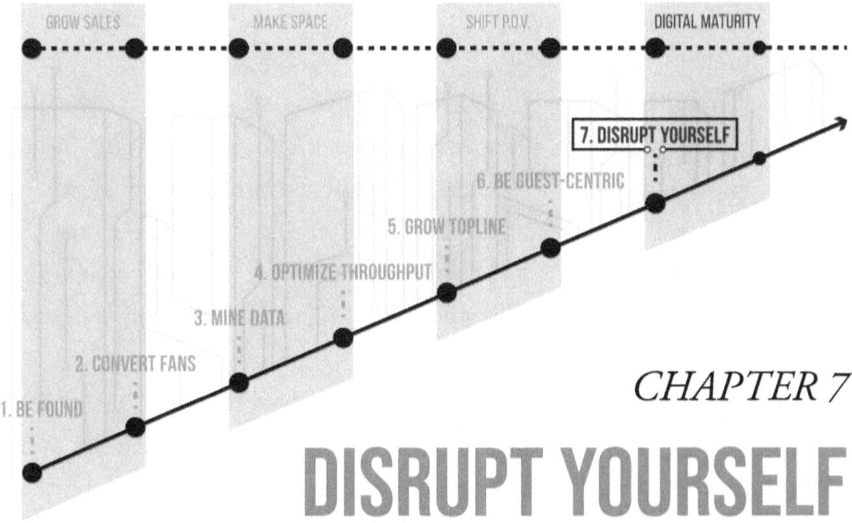

CHAPTER 7

DISRUPT YOURSELF

Kizzy had eagerly awaited this moment: a chance to visit Kevyn's new restaurant. She rarely got to this side of town, but since the article in the local press talked about Kevyn's success, she knew she had to see it for herself. It had already been a few months since his doors had opened. Today was the first chance that Kevyn had gotten to show Kizzy around.

"There you are!" He smiled, arms held aloft to embrace his friend. "I can't wait to show you this."

"I can't wait either. I tried to Google you to see some pictures, to check out the decor, and see what customers had to say after coming to your opening night. But I didn't find any pictures…I didn't even see any reservation listings," Kizzy replied with a quizzical look to her friend as he took her by the arm and crossed the street from her parked car.

"That, my dear Kizzy, is because this isn't any normal restaurant. This is a delivery-only restaurant," Kevyn said excitedly as he gestured toward the building.

"This…is your new restaurant?" asked an increasingly puzzled Kizzy. In front of her was a plain-looking building. There was no outdoor seating, no branding, no….anything, really. Just a two-way swing door that Kevyn pushed through, inviting his friend to follow. "You've built a ghost kitchen?" asked Kizzy.

"Well, yes and no," responded Kevyn. "I've vertically integrated a delivery restaurant. I have 8 new brands including Louis's from my other place, and I'm utilizing this tech package that connects it all together. And I can run it all right from here." Kevyn beckoned Kizzy over to look beside him as he demonstrated the operating system that ran his restaurant—all from a simple tablet very similar to the one she watched a movie on the previous night.

On the screen in front of them, Kevyn showed the locations of his drivers (and cyclists) and the time frames associated with their arrivals. With a swipe to the left, the screen brought up the KDS linking the kitchen activity and orders to the available logistical capability.

"This is going to be a long lunch, Kevyn. What have you gone and done now?" smiled Kizzy. Her friend was doing what he had done even back in their days together at school: breaking something and putting it back together while making it better than it was before.

Independent Restaurants: Disruptors or Disrupted?

The history of the restaurant industry is full of disruption. The drive for greater convenience through delivery and frictionless digital engagement are the latest disruptions, but they are not the first—and they are likely not the last. Disruption in the past has been all about bringing more value to the guest, where value is a unique mix of price, quality, convenience, choice, and experience.

Historically, independent restaurants have primarily been the victims of disruption. Chains were able to master the economic model, the consistency, the repeatability of development, and the scale of national advertising while independent restaurants could not. The result was a stagnant pool of independent restaurants—about 350,000 of them in the United States—while chain restaurants grew. As a result, the percentage of total American restaurants made up of American independents has declined over the last 30 years. As recently as the late 1990s, independent restaurants made up two-thirds of restaurants. Today, chains make up the majority of locations. A few notable chains are in decline, but due to the inertia of the brand, the moat of the real estate, the debt-leverageable free cash flow, and the fully depreciated assets, even underperforming chains have tended to stick around as zombie brands (in decline, but not going away).

And yet the restaurant guest is more excited to spend money with independents than with chains. A survey conducted in 2022 that included a thousand guests suggested that 65 percent of guests feel better about buying from local restaurants than chains.[51] Clearly, although chains are out-growing independents, independents have shown great staying power.

Organizations that found a winning, scalable formula—and copy/pasted that formula across the population—embodied each of the major restaurant types. Winning chains have become more prevalent in the United States than other Western countries due to more rapid population growth and more space available to develop. In countries such as Spain, the vast majority of restaurants are independents. Tourism dominates seventy percent[52] of Spain's GDP, and variety is most definitely the spice when on vacation—but the population growth rate[53] and available land to develop is far less than that of the US on both counts.

Whether you're an independent restaurant in the United States or one supporting the tourists visiting Spain, the challenges of disruption remain consistent. How can you add more value to the consumer experience in a way that can compete with chains? Will an independent restaurant be the one to define the next winning value equation, becoming a chain we have not yet even heard of? Will another restaurant model emerge that enables both chains and independents to successfully compete in the future for the attention of hungry diners?

To examine this further, let's take a moment to consider what has driven disruption in the US restaurant industry over the last hundred years. Each successive wave of disruption to the industry changed the value equation of a prepared meal for the guest. Comparing fine dining to QSR to casual dining to fast-casual shows the evolution of what consumers care most about. As each successive wave of disruption was perfected, it drove building activity, business formation, and disruptive destruction in ways that are indicative to what might happen next. Typically, in the past, a few restaurants would nail the formula and expand, becoming chains. Most independents, meanwhile, have stayed firmly in the dine-in or counter-style of restaurant.

A Step Back to Look Forward

Early restaurants offered a great experience in the form of full-service: diners, supper clubs, fine dining, and hotels. All restaurants were sit-down and full-service for many years. Counter service at drug stores began in the 1920s, which in many ways became a precursor to sandwich shops and delis. Next, drive-ins emerged with the adoption of automobiles. And then, at first slowly as several restaurants experimented with the model, and then all at once as the model was perfected, came the quick-serve restaurant (QSR), also known as fast food or drive-thru. The proliferation of QSRs certainly was associated with the car culture of the 1960s (cruising) and subsequent buildout of suburban neighborhoods. But QSR also proliferated because of simple price and speed. What had been expensive (fine dining with the associated elegant decor, expensive real estate, and trained servers) became affordable and convenient. What QSR did that no other restaurant had figured out was how to make restaurant-prepared food accessible to almost everyone.

In 2020 dollars, a typical QSR meal, complete with entree, side, and drink, could be purchased for about seven dollars. In the QSR model, 30 percent of the purchase price is directly attributable to food costs. So for that seven dollars, a consumer is receiving just over two dollars in food. Compared to fine dining, where the average meal is closer to forty dollars, and 20 percent of the purchase price typically goes to food costs, a consumer gets eight dollars' worth of food for forty dollars. The dining experience of a QSR meal is clearly meant to be fast, whereas the full service model is purposefully measured. QSR is providing the customer both value and convenience. Clearly, these are very different experiences meant for different consumer segments on different occasions, but the comparison is stark. For six times the price, a consumer at a full-service restaurant gets less than four times the food at a slower pace.

After QSR, delivery-only pizza emerged. As we discussed in Chapter 5 of the first *Delivering the Digital Restaurant*, Domino's created essentially the first ghost kitchen—a restaurant completely optimized for off-premise consumption. With its first location opening in 1960, Domino's became a national contender in the 1980s and an international one in the early 2000s. Soon after, other delivery-optimized pizza concepts followed. What was it about a delivered pizza that people loved so much? Yes, pizza is delicious. But the low price, coupled with delivered convenience, make it a tremendous value equation. For less than twenty dollars, a pizza can feed an entire family…without anyone even having to leave the house.

Casual dining was the next big wave of restaurant development. Taking our example again in today's dollars, a typical meal might be priced at twenty dollars and provide about five dollars and forty cents in food to the consumer. By paying twice what they were paying at QSR, consumers could get nearly twice the food and in addition, sit down and talk to one another while a server took orders and brought food. Comparing this model to the other sit-down, server-enabled model— fine dining—the reason casual dining took off becomes obvious: For half the price, consumers could get two-thirds the food and nearly as good of an experience.

Then, in the early 2000s, a new category emerged: fast-casual. The insight that drove fast-casual was this: Consumers wanted more variety than QSR menus—designed for speed and price—could offer, but they wanted it faster than casual dining could deliver. In fact, for that usage occasion, consumers preferred directly communicating their personalized orders to table service. In many ways, table service actually made consumers anxious, especially at lunch when guests had limited time available to eat. Could consumers trust the server to take their order, bring the food, and cash out the bill in the amount of time they had between meetings or off the clock? To put these fears at ease, many chain casual-dining concepts actually started to offer time guarantees at lunch.

Fast-casual took a different approach, and their strategy worked. The model eliminated servers, assigned seating, and dinnerware altogether, then reinvested the savings in the main thing consumers do care about: the food. At a typical price of twelve dollars for a meal, the consumer receives nearly

	DINE-IN	QSR	DELIVERED PIZZA	CASUAL DINING	FAST CASUAL
CONSUMER PRICE	$40	$7	$20	$20	$12
F&P %	20%	30%	25%	27%	32%
CONSUMER FOOD RECEIVED	$8	$2.10	$5	$5.40	$3.84
ORDER-TO-GUEST MINUTES	15-20	<5	30-45	10-15	<10
EXPERIENCE	X			X	X
QUALITY	X	X		X	X
VARIETY	X			X	X
PRICE		X	X		X
CONVENIENCE		X	X		

Figure 7.1 Restaurant Category Business Models

four dollars in food. For 60 percent of the price of casual dining, and just 20 percent more than QSR, fast-casual delivered higher quality food than both. At the same time, the consumer was evolving to care more about the nutrition and flavor of food. [For more on this, read Chapter 2 "Our Tastes Are Changing" in the first *Delivering the Digital Restaurant*.]

As a result of these successive waves of disruption, full-service restaurants have lost share in the industry. While the overall number of full-service restaurants has grown over the years, their percentage of restaurant locations has declined as each successive wave of restaurant model has emerged.

Innovation cycles happen swiftly in the restaurant industry. While it took 100 years to get to the first QSR drive-thru from a dine-in restaurant, delivered pizza came only about 20 years later. Casual dining arrived 20 years after that, with fast-casual close on its heels. Fast-casual has now been in place for over 20 years, and the time for the next big wave has come.

The Next Disruption: The Digitally Native Restaurant

What comes after fast-casual? The next big restaurant category is approaching, combining ghost kitchens, virtual brands, digital engagement, delivery fulfillment, electric cooking, intelligent software automation, and hardware robotics. Crucially, it will service all five value levers better than previous restaurant categories have done. The value, speed, variety, and quality it will offer—and the interface serving that up—will provide an experience like no other. We believe this new category will be known as "The Digitally Native Restaurant."

This category is still emerging because restaurants must completely reinvent their business model, mindset, and approach to fully realize the benefits of these new tools. When it is fully developed, like QSRs, the Digitally Native Restaurant will come suddenly and spread widely. It is so different from what exists today, with a radically different consumer proposition, that this category has the potential not just to replace existing independent restaurants, but to replace chains as well. Old business models do not compete well with new ones.

Other industries have already dealt with how digitization impacts business models: the travel, retail, and consumer goods industries have all incorporated digital into their business models, resulting in radical change.

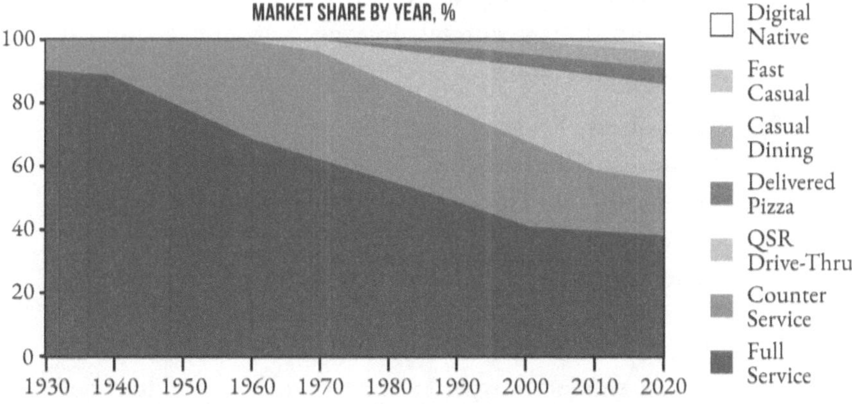

Source: Author estimates based on NPD Press Releases, QSR Top 50, FSR Top 50, Restaurant-ingthroughhistory.com, US Census Bureau

Figure 7.2 US Restaurants by Format

Travel responded to the disruption by going through massive consolidation to leverage the cost of innovative technology across more seat miles and room nights. Retail created an entirely new category—e-commerce—that has been dominated by a purpose-built, vertically-integrated behemoth called Amazon and has led to the demise of more than a few storied retailers. Consumer goods have experienced an explosion of "digital-native brands."

The digital-native brands (DNVB) in consumer goods can teach restaurants a lot about what the future model will look like. These brands, defined by Warby Parker CEO Andy Dunn in an essay on DNVBs, are "born on and primarily experienced via the internet [and] feature a vertically oriented business model which combines the margin of the retailer and brand."[54]

Digital-native brands offer consumers five benefits in their own unique value equation:

1. **& 2. Low Price for Level of Quality.** Digitally native brands reinvested costs from items consumers care less about (e.g., a retail footprint, salespeople) to the things they care more about (e.g., digital self-service, delivery convenience, lower price, and/or better product). Mattresses are a great example here. Where historically a new foam mattress might cost thousands of dollars when purchased in a retail store from a commission-based salesperson, a digitally-native foam mattress costs under a thousand dollars through internet self-service shipped directly to your door.

3. **Personalized Variety.** Digitally native brands utilize software intelligence and cloud computing to target ideal consumers. Once the consumer is on the website, recommendation engines further personalize their online experience (e.g., customized marketing offers, customization of product, cart-recovery discounts, subscription delivery). These tools enable a 1:1 relationship, which drives an enhanced experience beyond that of old-school loyalty programs and point collection programs.

4. **Frictionless Convenience.** Digitally native brands offer a fast, seamless consumer journey from exploration to

ordering, to delivery, returns, and issue resolution.

5. **Digital Experience.** Digitally native brands take advantage of user interfaces that could only exist online to create brand engagement. The online retailers make the purchase journey differentiated, too. Warby Parker's virtual try-on program is a great example of solving an old dilemma ("Do these glasses look good on me?") in a new way ("See yourself in anything, share some photos with your friends, then try on your favorites at home").

Like DNVBs in apparel and consumer packaged goods, the Digitally Native Restaurant will reorient how the consumer's dollar is spent to bring more value. A Digitally Native Restaurant will conveniently deliver a variety of high-quality meals for an unbelievable price, all through a seamless

	DINE-IN	QSR	DELIVERED PIZZA	CASUAL DINING	FAST CASUAL	DIGITAL NATIVE
CONSUMER PRICE	$40	$7	$20	$20	$12	$12
F&P %	20%	30%	25%	27%	32%	40%
CONSUMER FOOD RECEIVED	$8	$2.10	$5	$5.40	$3.84	$4
ORDER-TO-GUEST MINUTES	15-20	<5	30-45	10-15	<10	<30
EXPERIENCE	X			X	X	X
QUALITY	X	X		X	X	X
VARIETY	X			X	X	X
PRICE		X	X		X	X
CONVENIENCE		X	X			X

Figure 7.3 Restaurant Category Business Models

digital interface. Just as has been the pattern in restaurants for the last one hundred years, this new category will outgrow the others because it brings more value to the consumer. Imagine a restaurant that provided four dollars of food to the consumer for just ten dollars. Then, imagine if that food were conveniently delivered and available via a frictionless order process. Finally, imagine if that food were fresher, hotter, and higher quality without charging service fees for delivery. How would such a restaurant accomplish this feat and still make money?

While the appearance of "virtual restaurant brands" feels like the emergence of digitally native brands in restaurants, truly Digitally Native Restaurant concepts are still relatively rare. "Digitally native vertical brands are maniacally focused on the customer experience, and they interact, transact, and story-tell to consumers primarily on the web," says Warby Parker's Andy Dunn.[55] Virtual restaurant brands, for the most part, currently leverage third-party marketplaces to drive sales. As a result, they have very little brand storytelling, interaction, or customer experience. Most virtual brands do not even know who their consumers are, much less have a relationship with them. Most virtual restaurant brands are also dependent on their hosts (underlying brick-and-mortar restaurant). While these brands may add incremental revenue and profit to the restaurants from which they are fulfilled, their economics typically do not work on a standalone basis (nor are they meant to).

Digitally forward restaurants are taking the lessons from third-party SEO to make collections of virtual brands that work together. Brands like Salted, The Absolute Brands, Byte to Bite, Ghost Truck Kitchen, and Charlie Mae's use many different brands on many different marketplaces (or "digital storefronts," as Byte to Bite calls them) to drive sufficient revenue out of a single kitchen for the economics to work. Still, they rely heavily on the marketplaces.

Digitally Native: Purpose-Built Delivery-Optimized Restaurants

Delivering on the promise of a Digitally Native Restaurant requires rethinking everything. Start with a clean slate and build off a new foundation. Chapter 6 of the first *Delivering the Digital Restaurant* chronicles

Tip: Designing from a blank slate.

- A purpose-built, delivery-optimized restaurant is not how your current restaurant does delivery.

- Imagine how radically different a Domino's Pizza (the original ghost kitchen) was from the dine-in pizza restaurants at the time; that's how different a Digitally Native Restaurant is from a fast-casual or a QSR.

- Delivered pizza beat dine-in pizza because it designed everything around one objective: better-delivered pizza.

what we can learn from international markets because developing countries are in many ways ahead of the US in digital delivery. These countries can "skip the land line." Without a restaurant for every five hundred people (the US penetration) already built, these countries aren't constrained by making use of their existing restaurant infrastructure. These countries have more advanced digital ordering, digital payments, delivery networks, automation, and ghost kitchens.

Your restaurant is faced with a choice: start from first principles, and skip the land line or settle for delivery sales as an incremental bump on top of on-premise orders. Both are fine choices, but the Digitally Native Restaurant model will be higher-growth than traditional restaurants, even those that have gone all the way through the digital maturity path. As Digitally Native Restaurants increase perceived value by taking cost out of things consumers don't care about (labor, real estate) and investing the savings in things consumers do care about (food quality, price, delivery), they will become the high-growth concept of the restaurant industry.

Restaurants are already incredibly competitive and work diligently to continually remove costs all the time—but will these marginal changes ultimately help you disrupt yourself? This is where you face a decision point regarding the continuance of your journey to digital maturity. Do you want to continue to adjust your current model and do well but perhaps not as high-growth? Or do you want to reorient everything towards a new future?

The only way to achieve a truly different outcome is to start with first principles aimed at the new consumer demand. Asking the question, "If consumers want delivered food, what is the best way to get it to them?" will lead to new and different answers in both your business model and the technology that enables it.

Software entrepreneur turned restaurateur Chris Baggott sees the future this way:

> Sears had a catalog for well over 100 years before Amazon appeared. Sears invented the idea of shopping from home and having the goods come to the consumer. But they were disrupted when Amazon made the shopping experience and delivery logistics so good that consumers preferred the Amazon experience to going to a store. Amazon created this magical experience through exclusive focus on the delivery business and the technology to enable it. Catalog retailers lost the internet because they treated it as incremental rather than making it their core business. Amazon purpose-built a vertically integrated system that intertwined the physical world with the software one. Every physical action in the real world is matched by a virtual action in the software world. The software, being fully aware of every resource in the system, optimizes each and every step in the journey of the vendor, the consumer, and the product.[56]

In the case of Sears, Amazon's e-commerce mousetrap was so much better than shopping in-store that Sears actually declared bankruptcy and largely went away.[57] Many other brick-and-mortar retailers have gone out of business or shrunk their footprint in what's become known as "The Retail Apocalypse." While there have been a significant number of closures, brick-and-mortar has not gone away entirely—and the same will be true in restaurants. Just as drive-thrus did not replace dine-in restaurants, nor delivered pizza replace drive-thrus, the next wave of growth will not replace existing restaurant categories. "If I want a nice dinner, then I'm going to a restaurant," Baggott says of the need for specialized experiences. "If I want a drive-thru, then I'll go to a drive-thru when I'm out and about. But if I want food delivered to me, it's going to be better if it's purpose-built and focused around delivery."[58]

What delivery-optimized Digitally Native Restaurants will do is be the go-to for delivered food. Just as delivered pizza is optimized for delivery in everything—its location, its buildout, its packaging, its consumer interface—so too will delivery-centric Digitally Native Restaurants. There is an entire cuisine type that has this channel figured out. The next wave of growth in the restaurant industry will apply the lessons of pizza to other cuisine types.

But to enable any of this to happen, we must turn our attention away from what restaurant executives must do to reach maturity. At this juncture, the focus should be on what the technology companies must do to help restaurants reach their optimal digital capability, and that's what we'll cover next.

SUMMARY: DISRUPT YOURSELF

- Each disruption to the restaurant industry has changed the prepared meal value equation for guests.

- As different restaurant categories emerged, they enhanced value in the categories of Experience, Quality, Variety, Price and Convenience in different ways.

- The next disruption for restaurants will be through a new category: The Digitally Native Restaurant.

- The Digitally Native Restaurant will offer low price for quality, personalized variety, frictionless convenience and a digital experience that is differentiated from all other channels.

- Restaurant executives face a choice at this juncture a) to rethink their entire business model to embrace this new category and the growth potential it offers or b) settle for the stage of digital maturity that has been achieved in balancing the delivery channel alongside non-digital activity.

  **TIME FOR REFLECTION!**

CHAPTER 7: DISRUPT YOURSELF

1. Where do you see yourself on the digital maturity path today? How long has it taken to get there? Where do you see your restaurant in 2 years time? In 5 years?

2. What is the biggest challenge for your restaurant in developing greater digital maturity? Try the "3 Whys" technique: explain why you feel it is the biggest challenge. Then ask yourself "why" again? Repeat this process one last time. This will get you closer to the root challenge holding you back.

3. What steps can you take to address those challenges?

4. What is the best next step for your restaurant on the path to digital maturity?

5. Consider the next restaurant category that will capture the highest growth in the industry. Implicit in the Digitally Native Restaurant is a need to rip up the business model to increase value across all five levers (experience, quality, variety, price, and convenience). Can you see yourself taking that step? Why? Why not?

6. What costs would your restaurant have to eliminate or radically reduce to profitably serve consumers at 40 percent food costs?

7. Finally, what would you need to learn, build, or buy to underpin the new model?

8. If you don't see yourself adopting this new approach, how would what you wrote above affect your current restaurant if you took lessons from it?

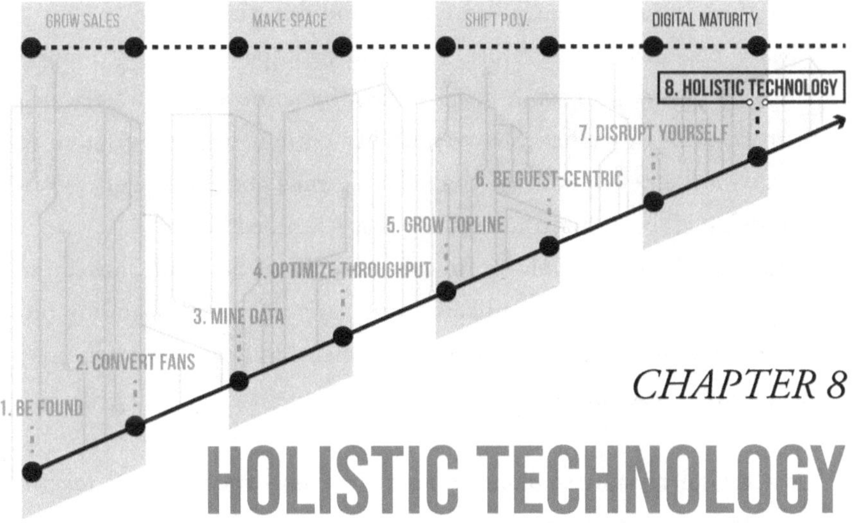

CHAPTER 8

HOLISTIC TECHNOLOGY

Josh peeked over the tablet station. Kizzy stood with her head tipped to one side, staring at one of the videos playing on loop. Josh made his move. She looked like just the right target profile to kick off Day 2 of the Phoenix conference after his team landed a record number of leads on Day 1.

"Can I help you?" he asked, followed by a quick smile with eyebrows raised.

"I don't really know. Can you?" replied Kizzy. She was already tired and had spent most of the prior day feeling bewildered by the complexity involved in digitizing Kwixo.

"Well, what are you looking for?" asked Josh, reaching towards a tablet, intending to scan Kizzy's badge so the team could follow up.

"I'm trying to boost my ability as a digital restaurateur, but it seems to me that each of you guys here claim to do everything. You make it all sound so easy, but…you all describe the opportunities in different ways, so it can't be easy."

Josh had heard this before. It's not like he could do anything about it—that was the product team's department. He spent the next 7 minutes going through his discovery process while sprinkling all the trimmings of product features, open API promises, and free trials.

Kizzy had heard this before, too. She had spent those 7 minutes half-listening to Josh while wondering why someone hadn't yet tied all these things together. She wanted her current technology suite to work with the new functionality she had learned about during her visit. Couldn't it all be better connected so that it worked better?

She smiled, nodded politely to Josh, took the leaflet, and allowed her badge to be scanned. She walked on towards the people handing out free samples of tiramasu. "Now this is something I can most definitely review and assess right here and now," she thought.

Most digital restaurant pioneers have Frankensteined (pieced together) their digital footprint through a combination of legacy technology, custom software development, and newer cloud-based software. Even more nimble independent restaurants are often faced with the choice of using software for something it isn't quite made to do, or not having the functionality at all.

Most restaurants at this stage are likely to spend 2 to 4 percent of sales on technology, excluding third-party commissions and credit card processing. It is a whopping amount, considering just 10 years ago most restaurants bought some POS hardware upfront and paid a small maintenance fee, and that was it. Worse, the cost of so many different pieces of software, and the upkeep associated with each one, is hidden so deep in the P&L of a restaurant that many do not even know what they are spending on technology. Some of those costs are capitalized; some are expensed. Some of the costs are at the restaurant level, some at headquarters. Some of the costs are software subscriptions, some are people. Some software is a regular monthly fee, but some is utility-based, and may cost less or more depending on the volume of transactions the software is handling.

For the most mature digital restaurants, those who seem to have everything figured out, the complexity only grows. Each problem solved unveils a new problem to be solved. And as diligent teams look to solve each problem, another layer of technology is added to the system.

Keeping track of what each piece of software does, training the restaurant on using it, ensuring the employees continue to use it, updating the software and its integrations, managing security for employee onboarding and offboarding… All of those things require full-time staff to oversee at a chain, or at least one dedicated person at an independent restaurant. For many independent owners and chain executives, the tech stack is now becoming a very heavy burden of semi-utilized tools that don't necessarily play well together.

Much as restaurants may need to re-think their business model to harness most optimal growth, technologists may have to reconsider their approach to designing the infrastructure that will ultimately enable the restaurant industry to reach its digital zenith. The end of the digital maturity path requires innovative restaurants and innovative technology companies. Restaurants with the will, budget, integrity, and vision to drive towards the final stage of digital maturity will rely on the technology companies that have got them this far to take them even further.

A typical, digitally mature restaurant needs 15 to 20 different pieces of software to run well, excluding third-party marketplaces. All this software must perform six major functions well, with sub-functions and optional features under each. These six functions are:

1. **General Management:** accounting, labor scheduling and payment, inventory and payment, vendor management

2. **Culinary Operations:** recipe management, inventory ordering, prep cycles

3. **Order Fulfillment:** meal preparation and expediting

4. **Logistics Management:** driver fleet management, order routing, batching

5. **Ordering & Channel Management:** menu management, pricing, order & pay from multiple consumer endpoints

6. **Loyalty & Marketing:** CDP, loyalty program, personalization engine, customer acquisition, customer remarketing

Historically, the general management and culinary operations functions have been handled by accounting or back-of-house software. Order fulfillment has been handled by a KDS (kitchen display system). Ordering and

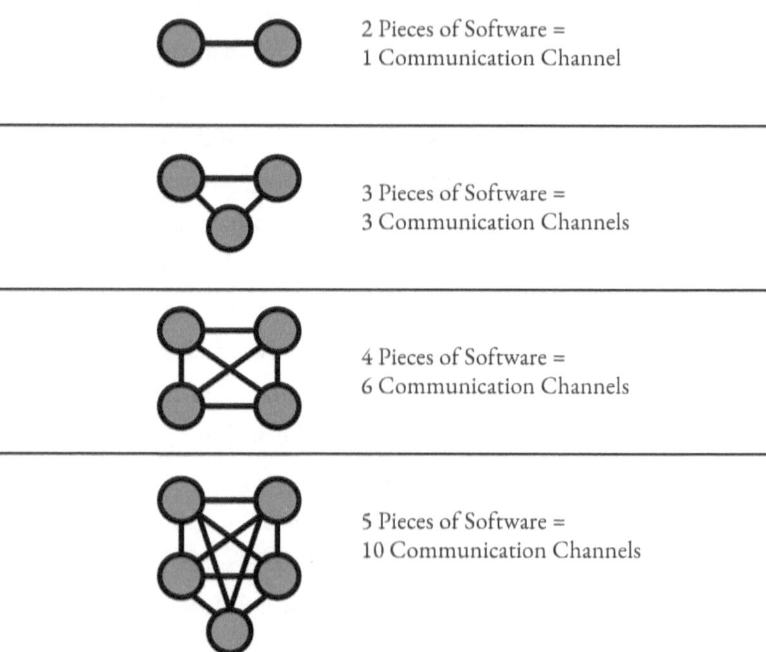

Figure 8.1 Compounding Complexity

channel management has been handled by the POS (point of sale). Logistics Management has been outsourced. Loyalty and marketing has been handled through expensive loyalty programs, where the cost of the software itself is only a tiny fraction of the compensation brands offer their consumers through discounts in order to get their data. Historically, some of these programs could speak to others creating a seamless process. Some did not.

As restaurant technology—and the demands placed on it by consumers, employees, and executives alike—became more sophisticated, the relationships between all of these functions grew more complex. Due to the rule of combinatorial explosion, where communication lines grow exponentially faster as each new piece of software is added to the tech stack, organizations have had to make choices between speed, simplicity, cost, functionality, and automation.

What if one piece of technology could accommodate most or all of these functions? One-system functionality, or holistic technology, enables everything from an order being placed all the way through to the optimized management of the workflow to fulfill the order and get it to its destination. Rather than a culinary operations software handing off information to an order fulfillment software, which is also taking in information from ordering and channel management and then giving information out to logistics management and loyalty and marketing, all of which is tracked by the accounting software…What if all these pieces could be reoriented into one system? In other industries, all of these functions are played by three major pieces, working together: a CRM (customer relationship management software), an ERP (enterprise resource planning software) and an OMS (order management system software).

CRMs are marketing technology that automates customer acquisition and remarketing by first tracking customer behavior, then segmenting customers and potential customers. An OMS takes orders from any input (mobile, app, kiosk, voice, POS) and routes it where it needs to go. ERPs are operations technology that automates operations decisions by coordinating resources. A restaurant ERP plus a restaurant CRM plus a restaurant OMS creates the powerful combination of a restaurant operating system (OS).

The CRM (customer relationship management) components automate customer acquisition/ remarketing through first tracking customer behavior and then segmenting customers to specific marketing strategies;

The OMS (order management system) channels orders appropriate to the restaurant's capability to execute and then communicates back to the consumer before the order is even completed;

The ERP (enterprise resource planning) system determines and distributes available resources (ingredients, equipment, labor, drivers) to best optimize the most expeditious pathway to complete an order.

You may, at this juncture, say that your POS provider offers all this today. Certainly, several of the major players are attempting to combine the technology features required to run a truly digital restaurant into one single system. In the world of software, this is called "Vertical SaaS," and it means that a single software company (SaaS) delivers everything needed for an operator in an industry (a vertical) to run effectively.[59]

The restaurant industry is still at the front end of digitization. This stage of disruption in an industry typically results in an explosion of innovation and a race to combine the elements that turn out to be the most valuable. Remember, at the beginning of the disruption, no one is entirely sure what consumers, employees, and executives will most want. New companies develop their MVPs (minimum viable products), then test and refine until it becomes clear what functionality is in high demand. Many companies are created. Few companies leap out ahead of the others as clear winners. Some companies don't make it. Some are purchased by the winners to become part of a larger system. Creative destruction is active in this phase of disruption.

Toast, for example, started its journey as a POS that enabled better, cheaper technology for independents by putting POS functionality in the cloud, charging a low monthly fee, and subsidizing its business model through payment processing fees. Today, they're acquiring new functionalities to be more than just a POS. "Our systems are wide and deep," Toast's CEO, Chris Comparato, said in an interview with Business Insider. "And we want restaurants to put that architecture at the center of their digital operation."[60] "Toast is replacing multiple vendors for loyalty, payroll, gift cards, and online order," Comparato told investors in the company's fourth-quarter earnings call.[61] The Toast CEO agrees we're in the early innings of innovation, and as a result, restaurant tech is "highly fragmented" with "a lot of point solutions."[62] By point solutions, Comparato means software that offers single or limited functionality, and must be combined with other pieces of software offering limited functionality in order to execute the desired outcome.

Restaurant365 began with accounting and has steadily built or bought functionality to include labor scheduling, culinary operations, and vendor management. CEO Tony Smith says, "Anything we think can become 10 percent or more of our overall revenue, we want to own that ourselves. The rest will be partners. We have a huge partner network. Just in POS, we import data from more than 100 POSs every day."[63]

The beauty of partnering for or acquiring functionality is that these large platforms with thousands of users can offer new modules to existing customers. For example, Toast says it has about seven percent of the restaurants in America using its POS. Rather than individual point solutions attempting to sell into 62,000 restaurants on their own, Toast can offer

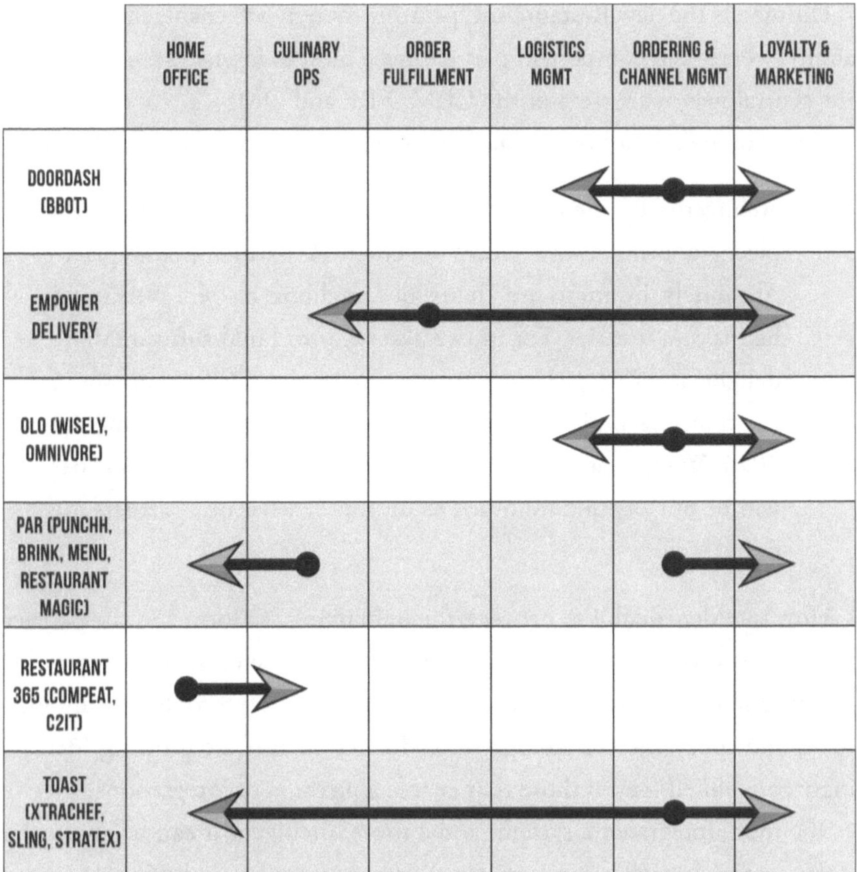

Figure 8.2 RestTech Players Pursuing a Restaurant Operating System

new solutions and partner products to existing customers. This dramatically lowers the customer acquisition cost—a main cost of SaaS software solutions.

Several other leading restaurant software vendors are pursuing a full restaurant OS, each starting from their heritage. Juan George, who built Olo's go-to market strategy, calls this era a "digital arms race."[64] While the last ten years have pushed restaurants toward open API architecture, where each piece of functionality can share data with the others, the next ten years will see the many point solutions either being subsumed into larger platforms or becoming "features as a service" that integrate into those platforms. Some providers in the US currently consolidating the ResTech space are Restaurant365, DoorDash, Olo, Toast, and Par.

Ultimately the new Restaurant Operating System will enable interdependability, where each component part has been built to interact seamlessly with the central nervous system of the CRM, ERP and OMS.

Comparato does not believe all functionality has to be in-house. If Toast is

> architecturally the best centerpiece, we're the connected centerpiece to bring those pieces together. A partner marketplace? Absolutely. I want to use Thanx, or Lunchbox, or Olo. We should be making it easier. For us, we also want to build software that's delightful. We'll pick and choose our battles. Order and pay at the table we built in 2019. We launched it in the summer of 2020. We have a number of projects that we're working on that will be our organic innovations on top of what our partners are doing.

How interdependability between the underlying platform and the partner function is executed will ultimately determine the success of Comparato's intent. Interdependability is central to any form of complex technology suite, and today the technology suites for restaurants are growing increasingly convoluted—even those that enable a plethora of integrations.

The more integrated a system is, the more intelligent it can be about the different activities that can occur in different resources of the system at any given time. This type of resource-aware software intelligence, combined with more electric forms of cooking—like sous vide, smart ovens, and air fryers—are pre-conditions to kitchen automation. Today, restaurant software augments human workers, making them more efficient and effective. But just as self-driving cars that didn't make much sense with combustion engines are starting to become viable with electric ones, holistic software has the potential to plug seamlessly into electric kitchen equipment that can be controlled with 1s and 0s and be upgraded and improved upon over time through over-the-air cloud updates.

In a restaurant context, are Digitally Native Restaurants the equivalent of electric cars? Will they enable true digital maturity as a fully integrated operating system? We believe so. Meredith has spun out the software that powers the ClusterTruck ghost kitchen business into its own software company. Empower Delivery, the software company, is helping restaurants boost their capability and capacity to service digitally native brands in ghost kitchens. By integrating functionality through holistic technology, ghost kitchens operating on the Empower Delivery system eliminate latency. With no unnecessary wait time, consumers get their food faster and hotter, but the restaurant is also highly utilized. Higher utilization delivers higher profits. Co-Founder and CTO Dan McFadden explains,

> With every resource of the system aware of every other resource of the system, software can make decisions that historically a person made. We saw the expertise in the expo role as data: when to fire what item, how to coordinate stations in the kitchen, how to ensure enough ingredients were prepped…but not too many. Data is ideal for an automated system; the software can organize the data to organize the activity in the kitchen.[65]

It is only a matter of time before software is telling robots what to do, rather than people. Not entirely digitally native but strongly digital-forward brands like Chipotle and Sweetgreen handle much of their automation technology and all their integrations by building in-house solutions or strategic acquisitions. For example, Sweetgreen's purchase of Spyce is enabling their buildout of "pickup-only" locations managed through robotic kitchens capable of producing 350 bowls per hour.

Chipotle's launch of their CVC (corporate venture capital) "Cultivate Next" fund focuses on robotics automation, demonstrating how this fast-casual giant sees robotics as the next wave of innovation for restaurants. Hyphen is a startup backed through the Chipotle fund. Like Spyce, Hyphen automates the make-line process of meal assembly into a few seconds of minimal human involvement, with zero inconsistency on plating and portion accuracy. "Hyphen is reimagining the intersection between makelines and digital kitchens, with a focus on improving speed and order accuracy," said Curt Garner, Chief Technology Officer at Chipotle.[66] The Hyphen operating system also enables the same robotic functionality to be programmed via over-the-air updates, ensuring that new recipes and menus can be seamlessly disseminated across a network without lengthy communication and training programs.

In other digitized verticals like e-commerce and business-to-business sales enablement, adding functionality has become so easy that new startups now take an "API-first" approach. This approach is starting to be adopted in the restaurant tech eco-system as well. A good example of back-end functionality that can be applied to any front-end system is dynamic pricing.

Amidst the furor of off-premise and the growth of incremental revenues, the off-premise channel's profitability remains a challenge. The case for incremental profitability (laid out in Chapter 7 of *Delivering the Digital Restaurant*) becomes less clear when off-premise mix grows above 30 percent of sales. When looking broadly at all the technology fees, marketplace commissions, and digital advertising costs involved in bringing the off-premise channel together, the pie becomes split into ever thinner slices.

This challenge has occurred before in other industries. The travel industry, for example, has already made the digitization maturity journey. The rise of marketplaces (think Expedia and Kayak), first-party ordering (think Marriott. com), and other technologies have disrupted hotels and airlines in a similar (albeit slower) way compared to how restaurants have been affected. One function now commonplace in the travel sector is just emerging for restaurants— dynamic pricing. Ashwin Kamlani, CEO of Juicer, is bringing his background in travel e-commerce to build dynamic pricing functionality for restaurants.

Restaurants have struggled for a long time to price in an informed manner. Typically, most restaurateurs have a margin in mind and adjust their prices when labor, ingredients, or rent cost increases. Now through dynamic pricing, restaurants can change their prices based on an algorithmic forecasting tool that accommodates their sales performance profile (by month, by day, by the hour), while also taking into account weather patterns, competitor pricing, inventory costs, and more. Kamlani believes,

> The true value of dynamic pricing is not just the ability to price appropriately while driving greater levels of profitability, but that it can enhance the customer experience too. In quieter times, a normally over-burdened kitchen can make the most efficient use of its capacity, reduce wait times for consumers, and at the same time reduce the strain on restaurant staff.[67]

In 2022, Juicer demonstrated the prowess of its algorithm in trials in enterprise chains and smaller groups, proving sizeable top-line revenue and bottom-line margin improvements through off-premise channels. "We fully anticipate dynamic pricing to follow the same path as in the travel sector and become active across all channels and, in doing so, provide some much-needed relief and support to the busy peaks and tight margins that restaurateurs have to navigate today."

The technologies that supplement digital ordering through various API (application programming interface) integrations can capture data beyond their own function to inform capacity constraints, unexpected surges, and employee throttling. This data can inform decisions beyond that of the immediate feature. For example, imagine if two cooks call out ill at the same time. Do you shut your marketplaces off? Cordon off half your tables? Or do you adjust the price of items? With a two-way integration, the ERP can engage with the dynamic pricing algorithm to then change prices. Juicer is actively shaping its go-to-market strategy with an API-first approach in mind, recognizing the value that comes from the interdependent functionality harnessed by a larger host technology platform.

Increasingly, API-based aggregators are helping lots of different technologies automatically interconnect and talk to each other in real-time to achieve greater efficiencies of cost, time, and precision. These companies provide support to enable seamless, plug-and-play integrations across multiple software systems via an "Integration Platform as a Service" (iPaaS) approach. iPaaS provides connectivity between POS platforms and offers dozens of functional platforms such as loyalty, inventory management, back-end logistics providers, and accounting— all in addition to providing consumer-facing platforms like the third-party marketplaces.

Sriram Subramanian, Founder and CEO of ShoppinPal, an iPaaS integrator, gets worked up about the thought of a restaurant dealing with the complexity of a convoluted tech stack. "Seamless integrations are a critical step in helping restaurants and retailers succeed with implementing technology quickly and effectively. We founded ShoppinPal to help well-developed but hitherto siloed tech functionalities talk to each other more effectively."[68]

As we have already indicated, the challenge with acquiring functionality is that each piece of software is architected and built differently. Although the open APIs allow an easy exchange of data, they do not always enable each function to make decisions based on what is happening in other functions. As artificial intelligence (AI) becomes commonplace in restaurant tech, to provide its best insight, that AI not only requires full access to all functions but must also control them to make changes based on its learnings over time.

Increasingly, the best systems will integrate all the pieces that matter the most—speed, accuracy, quality, cost, and brand—when creating the customer experience. Have a top 5 percent customer who orders from you all the time? Let them skip the line. That requires the loyalty program to be integrated with the culinary operations system. Got a product that routinely gets delivered incorrectly? That requires the customer review system to be integrated with the menu management system. Is a menu item slowing down the kitchen and you're wondering if you should delete it? That means the culinary operations system must be integrated with the sales mix, the recipe card, and the loyalty program to determine how much it sells, how profitable it is, and if it is being repeat-ordered by the most loyal customers.

Today, large restaurant chains employ data analysts to manually link disparate data sources from unrelated systems together. Independent restaurants can't afford to do this. Even for the large chains that can, the analysis is always retrospective—it simply isn't possible for humans to connect the systems real-time, but technology can. With interdependability central to the technology's design, most restaurants will be positioned to extract more value from their cost to serve. That value will translate into better food, faster delivery, and a customer experience that is unmatched within the food delivery eco-system. And that is something we all (technology providers included) should be hungry for.

CONCLUSION

If a restaurant can rethink its entire business model to improve the guest's value equation (price, speed, quality, variety and experience), then the future could be particularly bright. This new category of restaurant is emerging. Many different entrepreneurs are attacking different aspects of this evolution—incorporating robotics and electric cooking into their kitchens, eliminating on-premise consumption altogether, creating first-party ordering and delivery experiences that trump the third-party versions. At what point will these experiments manifest into a high-growth category in the years ahead?

It is possible that independent operators will drive this future, much as was the case with past disruptions. McDonald's was small once; now it defines the fast food category. Applebee's was small once; now it defines the casual dining category. A restaurant owner, toiling away in obscurity, may be creating the next big thing as we write. Even more exciting, the shift to Software-as-a-Service (SaaS) may mean that many unique independent restaurants could individually create a category, remaining small and never becoming a chain.

It has long been a myth that independent restaurant people are not businesspeople. They are foodies. They are families. They are operators. But they are also businesspeople. They are first-class entrepreneurs who take risks, investing in a street corner to bring something new to their communities.

They innovate not just the menu and the decor, but also the service model and increasingly, the technology that supports it.

Most restaurants will follow the path to digital maturity and increasingly incorporate technology into their business. Some will go straight to the end game, employing holistic software and plugging in headless API commerce functions as they are invented.

We hope this book has not only enabled you to find your place on the journey to digital maturity, but also chart the path forward, guiding where you and your restaurant(s) will head in the years to come. There is an exciting path for all of us to follow. The Digital Restaurant train is coming, and all that's left for you to decide is whether you're coming along for the ride.

Endnotes

1   Author interview with Chris Comparato, March 14, 2022

2   Author interview with Barry Shuster, February 3, 2022

3   YipitData panel presentation at Food on Demand Conference, May 4, 2022

4   Andre Verner speaking at Food on Demand Conference, May 2022

5   Alonso Castenada speaking at Food on Demand Conference, May 2022

6   Chintan Zalani, "47 SEO Statistics for 2023," On the Map, January 4, 2023, https://www.onthemap.com/blog/seo-statistics/

7   Chintan Zalani, "47 SEO Statistics for 2023," On the Map, January 4, 2023, https://www.onthemap.com/blog/seo-statistics/

8   Brian Dean, "We Analyzed 4 Million Google Search Results," BACKLINKO, October 14, 2022, https://backlinko.com/google-ctr-stats

9   Christine Kilpatrick, "Digitizing the Kitchen: VCs Turn Up The Heat On Restaurant Tech Investment," Crunchbase, March 16, 2022, https://news.crunchbase.com/business/restaurant-tech-venture-capital-startups-cloudkitchens/

10   Author interview with Shawn Walchef, January 7, 2022

11   Author interview with Rev Ciancio, January 14, 2022

12   "Upselling and Cross Selling: Restaurant Examples for C-Stores to Follow," Bounteous, February 7, 2022, https://www.bounteous.com/insights/2022/02/07/upselling-cross-selling-restaurant-examples-c-stores-follow

13   "Alternative Payments: It's Time to Start Thinking Beyond Credit Cards," Chargebacks911, October 7, 2022, https://chargebacks911.com/alternative-payments/

14   "Consumer Research: Digital Payments Are in Demand—Is Your Restaurant Ready?" Bounteous, September 15, 2022, https://www.bounteous.com/insights/2022/09/12/consumer-research-digital-payments-are-in-demand

15   "2021 Restaurant Payments Insight Report," US Bank, 2021

16   "42% Of Consumers Say They'll Try Digital Wallets," PYMENTS, November 29, 2022, https://www.pymnts.com/travel-payments/2022/payments-and-treasury-platform-sunrate-partners-with-travel-app-agoda/

17   "Digital Maturity Benchmark Restaurant Industry 2022," Incisiv, 2022 https://www.incisiv.com/report-restaurant-industry-2022

18   "Consumer Research: Digital Payments Are in Demand–Is Your Restaurant Ready?" Bounteous, September 15, 2022, https://www.bounteous.com/insights/2022/09/12/consumer-research-digital-payments-are-in-demand

19   Jean Chick, "Beyond the Punch Card" Deloitte, December 2021, https://www2.deloitte.com/us/en/pages/consumer-business/articles/restaurant-loyalty-program.html

20   Author interview with Zach Goldstein, September 1, 2021

21   Robert Cialdini, Influence: The Psychology of Persuasion, Revised Edition, Harper-Business, 2006

22   Author interview with Tony Smith, January 28, 2022

23   Author interview with Abhinav Kapur, February 2, 2022

24   "11 Tips to Design a High Performing DoorDash Menu," Doordash, August 14, 2022, https://get.doordash.com/en-us/learning-center/maximize-your-menu

25   Author interview with Ellie Doty, December 17, 2022

26   "Restaurant Sales Remain Strong with Last Two Months Posting Highest Growth Since March," Black Box Intelligence, November 17, 2022,   https://blackboxintelligence.com/restaurant-sales-remain-strong-with-last-2-months-posting-highest-growth-since-march/

27   Amanda McNamara, "How to Reduce Restaurant Employee Turnover," Toast,

 https://pos.toasttab.com/blog/on-the-line/how-to-reduce-restaurant-employee-turnover-guide

28   D.J. Costantino, "The Great Resignation Is Here. What 3,700 Restaurant Employees Are Looking For to Stay Engaged," 7Shifts, December 13, 2021 https://www.7shifts.com/blog/restaurant-employee-engagement-study-and-survey/

29   D.J. Costantino, "How Andolini's Uses 7shifts to Help with Schedule Empathy: Case Study," 7shifts, August 27, 2021 https://www.7shifts.com/blog/how-andolinis-uses-7shifts-to-help-schedule-with-empathy/

30   D.J. Costantino, "How Chatime Canada Conquered Spreadsheet Mountain: Case Study," 7shifts, July 27, 2022 https://www.7shifts.com/blog/how-chatime-canada-conquered-spreadsheet-mountain/

31   Author interview with Jordan Boesch December 15, 2022

32   Andrew Robbins presentation at Global Restaurant Leadership conference, November 16th 2022

33   Global Restaurant Leadership conference, November 16th 2022, JW Marriott, Dubai

34   Author Interview with Brian Reece and Steve Crowley, October 7, 2022

35   Author interview with Moin Islam, January 13, 2022

36   Author Interview with Rishi Nigam, January 21, 2022

37   Author Interview with Stephanie Sollers, September 13, 2022

38   Author Interview with Dustin Mares, November 23, 2022

39   Author Interview with Atul Sood, August 29, 2022

40   Author interview with Chris Baggott, September 14, 2022

41   Sean Burch, "Americans Spend Record Six Hours-Plus Each Day on Digital Media, New Report Shows," The Wrap, June 11, 2019 https://www.thewrap.com/americans-6-hours-a-day-on-digital-media/

42   https://www.supplychaindive.com/news/walmart-fulfillment-center-tennessee-ai-robots-automation-shipping/611261/

43   https://www.supplychaindive.com/news/nordstrom-opex-omnichannel-fulfillment-technology/566077/

44   Author Interview with Ilir Sela, September 12, 2022

45   "Why Your C-Store Needs a Customer Data Platform," Bounteous, August 31, 2021, https://www.bounteous.com/insights/2021/08/31/why-your-c-store-needs-customer-data-platform

46   Author Interview with Abhinav Kapur, February 2, 2022

47   "The Ultimate Guide to Restaurant Email Marketing," DoorDash for Merchants, https://assets.ctfassets.net/trvmqu12jq2l/6uyReI3MdDaM9RcJxuTPMH/926662aa-d89e871cfc18d6e2457449f9/DoorDash-Ultimate-Guide-Restaurant-Email-Marketing.pdf

48   Author interview with Noah Glass, December 12, 2022

49   "Restaurant Readiness Index," Pymnts, 2022 https://www.pymnts.com/study/restaurant-readiness-metaverse-digital-innovation-order-ahead/

50   Julie Littman, "Why Chipotlanes Are Chipotle's Future," Restaurant Dive, November 21, 2022, https://www.restaurantdive.com/news/chipotlanes-are-chipotles-future/637022/

51   Alicia Kelso, "Survey: 65% of Consumers Prefer Local Restaurants over Chains," Restaurant Dive, May 26, 2022, https://www.restaurantdive.com/news/survey-nearly-two-thirds-of-consumers-prefer-local-restaurants/623862/

52   "Contribution of the Tourism Sector to the Gross Domestic Product of Spain 2006-2021," Statista, https://www.statista.com/statistics/640440/travel-tourism-total-gdp-contribution-spain/

53   "Spain Population Growth Rate 1950-2023," MacroTrends, https://www.macrotrends.net/countries/ESP/spain/population-growth-rate and "US Population Growth Rate 1950-2023," MacroTrends,

https://www.macrotrends.net/countries/USA/united-states/population-growth-rate

54   https://techcrunch.com/2016/07/05/startups-need-to-respect-the-laws-of-retail-physics/

55   Antonio Altamirano, "How to Build a Digital Native Brand," Forbes, September 14, 2018, https://www.forbes.com/sites/forbestechcouncil/2018/09/14/how-to-build-a-digital-native-brand/?sh=5e843f0019dc

56   Author interview with Chris Baggott, 15 September 2022

57   Erin McDowell and Avery Hartmans, "The Rise and Fall of Sears," Business Insider, December 19, 2022, https://www.businessinsider.com/rise-and-fall-of-sears-bankruptcy-store-closings#the-settlement-cleared-the-way-for-sears-to-emerge-from-bankruptcy-since-then-the-company-has-slashed-the-number-of-stores-nationwide-25

58   https://www.restaurantowner.com/public/Corner-Booth-Podcast.cfm Episode 54, "Chris Baggott."

59   Prithvi Manjunatha "What Is Vertical SaaS and Why It's the Future of SaaS," Saastitute, February 23, 2022, https://www.saastitute.com/blog/what-is-vertical-saas-and-why-its-the-future

60   Nancy Luna, July 2022, "Toast CEO is 'Laser-Focused' on the $65 Billion Restaurant Tech Space as It Scoops up Another Food Tech Startup and Expands Services," Business Insider, https://www.businessinsider.com/toast-ipo-chris-comparato-dominating-payment-processing-post-ipo-2022-7

61   Motley Fool Transcribing, "Toast, Inc. (TOST) Q4 2021 Earnings Call Transcript," Motley Fool, February 17, 2022 https://www.fool.com/earnings/call-transcripts/2022/02/17/toast-inc-tost-q4-2021-earnings-call-transcript/

62   Author interview with Chris Comparato, March 14, 2022

63   Author interview with Tony Smith, January 28, 2022

64   Author interview with Juan George, August 18, 2022

65   Author interview with Dan McFadden, January 2, 2023

66   "Chipotle Invests in Robotic Makeline and Plant-Based Protein Via It's New Venture Fund," July 21, 2022 https://ir.chipotle.com/2022-07-21-chipotle-invests-in-robotic-makeline-and-plant-based-protein-via-its-new-venture-fund

67   Author Interview with Ashwin Kamlani, October 6, 2022

68   Author interview with Sriram Subramanian, September 13, 2022

ABOUT THE AUTHORS

Carl Orsbourn and Meredith Sandland are co-authors of the award-winning book *Delivering the Digital Restaurant: Your Roadmap to the Future of Food*. They now bring you the follow-on book *Delivering the Digital Restaurant: The Path to Digital Maturity* to help guide restaurants step-by-step through the digital disruption. As active mentors to the industry, they have spoken at industry and private events around the world and both serve on the boards of restaurants and emerging technology companies. They host The Digital Restaurant podcast and are regular columnists in industry publications such as Nations Restaurant News and RestaurantOwner.com.

Carl and Meredith met at Kitchen United, the Google Ventures-backed ghost kitchen startup. At Kitchen United, Meredith created the concept and Carl the operating model. They saw first-hand how restaurants were trying to adapt to the rapid change brought on by consumer demand for delivery, increased restaurant technology, and disruptive business models like ghost kitchens and virtual brands.

Meredith and Carl are currently pursuing the latest innovation in restaurant technology. Meredith is the CEO of Empower Delivery, a SaaS company that enables delivery-centric restaurants to manage end-to-end delivery transactions—including the customer journey, the product journey, and the logistics journey—through one platform.

Carl is the COO of Juicer, a dynamic pricing company that enables restaurants to optimize their prices on digital channels through machine learning algorithms that incorporate a myriad of factors such as competitor price points, weather, and events.

Meredith and Carl were both recognized as Technology Power Players in 2021 and 2022 by Business Insider, and recognized by Nations Restaurant News and QSR Magazine for their thought leadership in supporting restaurants to adapt to the challenges and opportunities offered through digitization, technology, and automation.

Prior to their careers in restaurant technology, both Meredith and Carl were Fortune 500 executives—Meredith as Chief Development Officer at Taco Bell (part of Yum! Brands) and Carl as Head of Retail at ampm (part of bp).

DOWNLOAD THE **FREE** WORKBOOK COMPANION!

SCAN THE CODE TO ACCESS YOUR COPY